Practice Workbook

Scott Foresman - Addison Wesley

Editorial Offices: Menlo Park, California • Glenview, Illinois
Sales Offices: Reading, Massachusetts • Atlanta, Georgia • Glenview, Illinois
Carrollton, Texas • Menlo Park, California

http://www.sf.aw.com

Overview

Practice Worksheets provide additional exercises for students who have not mastered key skills and concepts covered in the Student Edition. A Practice worksheet is provided for each core lesson of the Student Edition. In addition, a Practice worksheet is also provided for each Mixed Practice and Cumulative Review lesson.

Lesson worksheets provide exercises similar to those in the Practice and Explore lessons of the Student Edition.

Mixed Practice worksheets review skills and concepts covered in the Student Edition section and include application problems that review previous material.

Cumulative Review worksheets cover important skills from the current chapter and from previous chapters.

ISBN 0–201–31243–3

Printed in the United States of America

3 4 5 6 7 8 9 10 – BW – 02 01 00 99 98

Contents

Chapter 10: Numbers to 1,000

Chapter 11: Measurement

Chapter 12: Geometry and Fractions

Chapter 13: Multiplication and Division Concepts

Name ______________________________

Practice
I-3

Skip Counting

I. How many mittens?

Count by 2s. Write the numbers.

 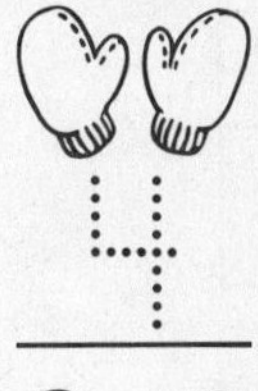  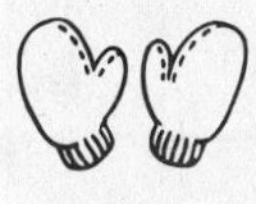  

2 ____ 4 ____ ____ ____ ____ ____

____ ____ ____ ____ ____ mittens

2. How many petals are on the flowers?

Count by 5s. Write the numbers.

____ ____ ____ ____ ____ petals

Count by 2s, 5s, or I0s. Write the numbers.

3. 6, 8, ____, ____, ____

4. I5, 20, ____, ____, ____

5. 20, 30, ____, ____, ____

6. 30, 32, ____, ____, ____

Problem Solving Estimation

How many fingers are there in your class?

Estimate the number of fingers.

Then count the fingers. Count by I0s.

7. Estimate: ____ fingers

8. Count: ____ fingers

Notes for Home Your child counted by 2s, 5s, and 10s. *Home Activity:* Ask your child to count 50 items, such as beans or macaroni, by 2s, 5s, and 10s.

Name ______________________________

Practice
1-4

Problem Solving: Look for a Pattern

Continue the patterns. Color the numbers.

1.

1	2	**3**	4	5	**6**	7	8	**9**	10
11	12	13	14	15	16	17	18	19	20
21	22	23	24	25	26	27	28	29	30
31	32	33	34	35	36	37	38	39	40
41	42	43	44	45	46	47	48	49	50

2.

1	2	3	4	5	**6**	7	8	9	10
11	**12**	13	14	15	16	17	**18**	19	20
21	22	23	24	25	26	27	28	29	30
31	32	33	34	35	36	37	38	39	40
41	42	43	44	45	46	47	48	49	50

Visual Thinking

3. Make your own pattern. Color to show how it begins.
Ask a friend to finish the pattern.

11	12	13	14	15	16	17	18	19	20
21	22	23	24	25	26	27	28	29	30
31	32	33	34	35	36	37	38	39	40
41	42	43	44	45	46	47	48	49	50
51	52	53	54	55	56	57	58	59	60

Notes for Home Your child continued number patterns. *Home Activity:* Ask your child to describe the pattern in each chart on this page. (Exercise 1: counting by 3s; Exercise 2: counting by 6s)

Name ______________________________

Mixed Practice: Lessons 1–4

1. Circle the color that has more cubes.

   white gray

2. Circle the color that has fewer cubes.

   white gray

Use the graph to answer the questions.

3. Are there more stars or moons?

   ____

4. How many more? _____ more

Stars	Moons
☆ ☆ ☆ ☆ ☆ ☆ ☆ ☆ ☆ ☆ ☆	☾ ☾ ☾ ☾ ☾ ☾ ☾ ☾

Count by 2s or 5s. Write the numbers.

5. 15, 20, 25, _____, _____, _____, _____, _____, _____

6. 6, 8, 10, _____, _____, _____, _____, _____, _____

Problem Solving

7. Continue the pattern. Color the numbers.

1	2	3	4	5	6	7	8	9	10
11	12	13	14	15	16	17	18	19	20
21	22	23	24	25	26	27	28	29	30

Journal

8. Draw a picture of 2 groups. Circle the group that has fewer.

Notes for Home Your child practiced comparing numbers and completing counting patterns. *Home Activity:* Ask your child to create a number pattern for you to continue. Then have him or her check your answers.

Name ______________________

Practice Chapter 1 A

Cumulative Review

Count how many. Write the numbers.

1. 

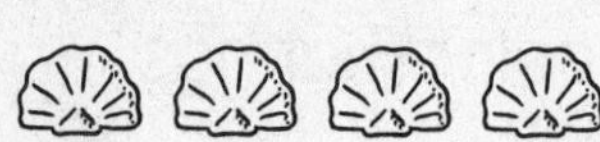

_____

2. 

_____

3. Which group has more, the whales or the shells?

____

4. How many more?

_____ more

5. Which name has more letters?

____

6. How many more? _____ more

Test Prep

Fill in the ○ for the correct answer.

7. What number comes next?

46, 47, 48, 49, _____

45	59	50	60
○	○	○	○

8. What number comes next?

53, 54, 55, 56, _____

57	59	60	66
○	○	○	○

Notes for Home Your child reviewed number groups to 9, sorting and classifying, and counting patterns.
Home Activity: Ask your child to say the next 5 numbers in Exercise 8. (58, 59, 60, 61, 62)

Name ______________________________

Practice 1-5

Graphs

Use the graphs to answer the questions.

1. How many children like peas?

 ______ children

2. How many more children like carrots than peas?

 ______ more

Which Vegetable Do You Like Better?	
Peas	4 peas
Carrots	7 carrots

3. Which sandwiches do an equal number of children like best? Circle the foods.

 Ham Turkey Cheese

4. Which sandwich was picked the greatest number of times?

 ____

What Is Your Favorite Sandwich?		
4 sandwiches	5 sandwiches	4 sandwiches
Ham	Turkey	Cheese

5. **Write your own** question about one of the graphs.

____

Problem Solving Estimation

5. Do you think more children in your class like peanut butter and jelly sandwiches or tuna fish sandwiches? Circle your estimate.

 peanut butter and jelly tuna fish

 You can make a graph to check your estimate.

Notes for Home Your child answered questions about graphs. *Home Activity:* Ask your child to make a graph like the one in Exercise 3 that shows family members' votes for favorite sandwiches.

Name ______________________________

Pictographs

Practice 1-6

Use the graph. Give each answer.

1. How many children like orange juice best?

   ______ children

2. Which fruit juice is the favorite of most of the children?

   ____

Favorite Fruit Juice	
Orange	☺ ☺ ☺ ☺ ☺
Apple	☺ ☺ ☺ ☺ ☺ ☺ ☺
Grape	☺ ☺ ☺

Each ☺ means 1 child.

Mixed Practice

Count by 2s to find each answer.

3. How many children like apple bread best?

   2 __ 4 __ ____ ____ ____

4. How many children like apricot bread best?

   2 __ 4 __ ____ ____ ____ ____ ____

Each [stick figure] means 2 children.

Mental Math

5. How many more children picked apple juice than grape juice in the graph above? ______

Notes for Home Your child answered questions about pictographs. *Home Activity:* Ask your child to think of a question that compares two items in one of the graphs. (Possible question: How many more children like banana bread than apple bread? (3))

Name ______________________________

Practice
1-7

Experiment and Tally

Karen tossed a 2-colored counter. Then she tallied her results. Count how many red, how many blue, and how many in all.

Red	Blue
|||	𝍸 𝍸 ||

Red	Blue
𝍸 ||	𝍸 |||

1. How many red? 3
2. How many blue? ______
3. How many in all? ______
4. How many red? ______
5. How many blue? ______
6. How many in all? ______

Show the tallies for each chart.

Red	Yellow

Red	Yellow
	/

7. Show 9 red.
8. Show 11 yellow
9. How many in all? ______
10. Show 11 red.
11. Show 18 yellow.
12. How many in all? ______

Problem Solving Critical Thinking

13. If you toss a number cube 20 times, could it land on six 20 times? Why or why not?

Notes for Home Your child read and made tally charts. *Home Activity:* Ask your child to tell you which tally chart shows the most yellow tosses and the fewest yellow tosses. (Most: lower right chart with 18 tosses. Fewest: lower left chart with 11 tosses.)

Name ______________________________

Practice 1-8

Bar Graphs

1. Do you live on a street, avenue or road? Ask 10 classmates. How many letters are there in each street name? Make tally marks.

Number of Letters in Our Street Names							
1	2	3	4	5	6	7	8
9	10	11	12	13	14	15	16

2. Make a bar graph. Color 1 space for each tally mark.

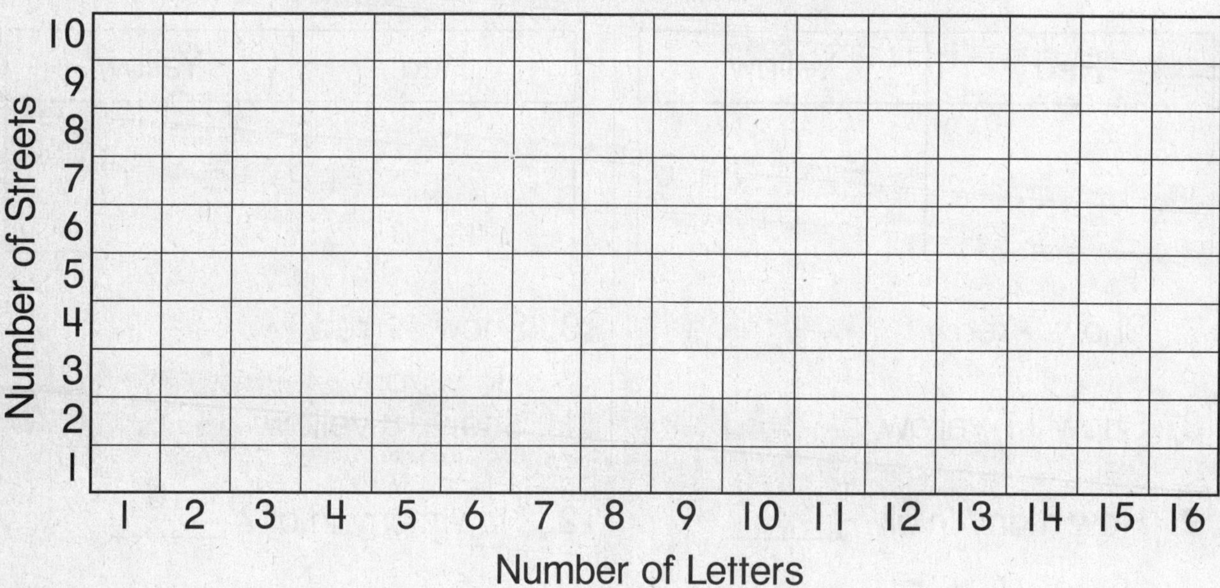

Problem Solving Critical Thinking

3. Suppose 8 children have 9 letters in their street names. Explain how you would show this on a bar graph.

Notes for Home Your child has gathered and shown data using tally marks and a bar graph. *Home Activity:* Ask your child to add the street names of family members including cousins, uncles, aunts, and grandparents.

Name ______________________

Problem Solving: Collect and Use Data

1. Show data for 8 classmates using a diagram.

Do You Like Roller Coasters or Water Slides?

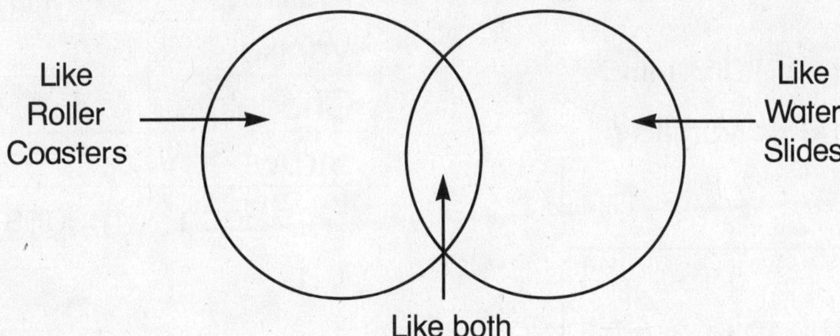

Use your diagram to answer the questions.

2. How many children like both roller coasters and water slides? ______

3. How many children like roller coasters? ______

4. How many children like roller coasters but not water slides? ______

5. How many children like water slides? ______

6. How many children like water slides but not roller coasters? ______

Tell a Math Story

7. Tell a short story about 7 friends. Ask a friend to draw a diagram for your story.

Notes for Home Your child collected, organized, and used data to solve problems. *Home Activity:* Work with your child to create a diagram like the one on this page that shows how many family members like bananas, grapes, or both.

Use with pages 25–26.

Name ______________________________

Practice
Chapter 1
B

Mixed Practice: Lessons 5–9

Use the graph. Solve.

1. How many children like strawberry best? ______

2. Do more children like chocolate or vanilla?

____

Favorite Milk Flavor	
Plain	▢▢▢▢▢
Vanilla	▢▢
Chocolate	▢▢▢▢▢▢▢▢
Strawberry	▢▢▢▢

Each ▢ means 1 child.

Use the graph to answer the questions.

3. Which soup was picked most often?

____

4. Which soup was picked least often?

____

Problem Solving

Look at the diagram. Answer the questions.

5. How many children like apples but not pears? ______

6. How many children like both apples and pears? ______

Likes apples
Likes pears
Likes both
Don
Kim Jane
Ellen
Bob
Jan
Anita
Theo

Journal

7. Write a question about the diagram. Ask a friend to answer your question.

Notes for Home Your child practiced using graphs to compare information. *Home Activity:* Have your child add his or her vote to the graph about a favorite soup. Ask: *Does this change the answers to Exercises 3 and 4?* (No, 1 vote for any soup would not change the answers.)

Name ______________________________

Cumulative Review

Circle the number that is greater.

1. 7 5

2. 10 16

Circle the number that is less.

3. 14 11

4. 8 6

Problem Solving

Solve.

5. There are 7 frogs.
There are 5 toads.
Which group has more?

____

6. There are 6 wasps.
There are 9 hornets.
Which group has fewer?

____

Test Prep

Fill in the ○ for the correct answer.

7. Count by 2s.
Mark the number that comes next.

2, 4, 6, 8, ______

○ 9 ○ 10 ○ 11 ○ 12

8. Count by 5s.
Mark the number that comes next.

10, 15, 20, 25, ______

○ 26 ○ 28 ○ 30 ○ 35

Notes for Home Your child reviewed comparing numbers and skip counting. *Home Activity:* Ask your child to assemble 2 groups of objects at home that are equal in number, and then create a third group with fewer objects.

Name ______________________________

Explore Addition Stories

Practice 2-1

8 .

Lea brings 2 more .

How many in all?

8 and 2 is 10.

Solve each problem. You can use .

1. 7 on a plate.

3 more 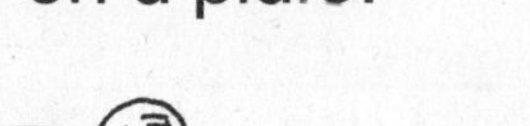 are added.

How many  in all?

_____ and _____ is _____.

2. 5 on Tim's plate.

4 on Kim's plate.

How many  in all?

_____ and _____ is _____.

3. 6 on the table.

2 more  are added.

How many  in all?

_____ and _____ is _____.

4. 3 on the table.

5 are added.

How many in all?

_____ and _____ is _____.

Talk About It Tell a classmate a number story about this picture.

Notes for Home Your child solved addition stories. *Home Activity:* Ask your child to tell you an addition story about 3 honey bees flying around and 4 honey bees on flowers.

Name ______________________________

Practice 2-2

Join Groups to Add

You can use ⬭ ⬭ and a ▭▭.

Write the number sentence. Solve.

1. 5 bees are in a hive.

   4 more bees join them.

   How many bees are there now?

   5 and 4 is 9 bees

2. 4 cats sit in the sun.

   3 cats join them.

   How many cats in all?

   _____ and _____ is _____ cats

3. 3 dogs are playing.

   5 more dogs also play.

   How many dogs in all?

   _____ and _____ is _____ dogs

4. 7 butterflies on the flowers.

   2 more butterflies come.

   How many butterflies are on the flowers now?

   _____ and _____ is _____ butterflies

Problem Solving Critical Thinking

5. Solve. You can use ⬭ ⬭.

   There are 9  in all. 

   How many cats are hiding under the blanket?

   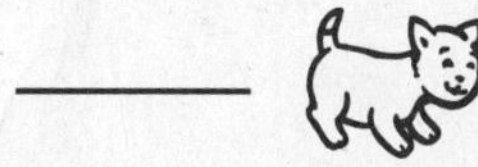

Notes for Home Your child wrote number sentences for addition stories. *Home Activity:* Ask you child to tell you an addition story and then explain how he or she would find the answer.

Name ____________________

Practice 2-3

Count On and Add Zero

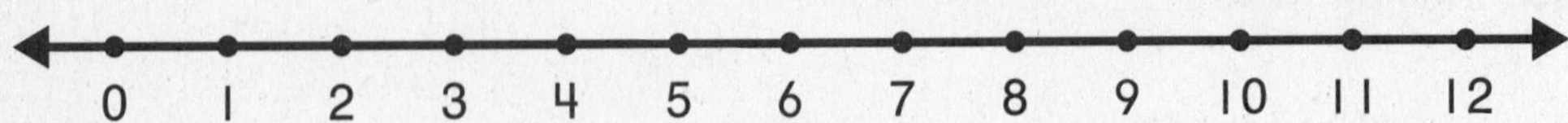

Use the number line. Write the sum.

1. 3 + 1 = 4   5 + 3 = ____
2. 8 + 0 = ____   9 + 2 = ____
3. 6 + 3 = ____   2 + 1 = ____
4. 1 + 2 = ____   2 + 0 = ____
5. 7 + 4 = ____   4 + 2 = ____

Add.

6. 8 + 1 = ____   1 + 2 = ____   6 + 3 = ____   5 + 0 = ____   3 + 3 = ____   9 + 2 = ____

7. 7 + 3 = ____   4 + 0 = ____   2 + 1 = ____   1 + 0 = ____   8 + 3 = ____   3 + 2 = ____

Problem Solving Critical Thinking

8. Start with 6. Add a number so that the sum is 6. What number did you add? ____

Notes for Home Your child added 0, 1, 2, or 3 to numbers. *Home Activity:* Show your child from 1 to 9 buttons or beans. Have your child use them to show you how many is 0, 1, 2, and 3 more.

Name ______________________

Practice 2-4

Turnaround Facts

Write the number sentence for each train.

1. 

3 + 5 = 8

5 + 3 = 8

2. 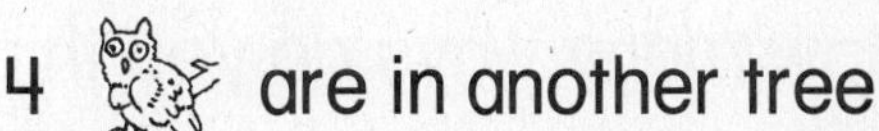

____

____

3.

____

____

4.

____

____

Write the turnaround fact for each number sentence.

5. 4 + 7 = 11

____

6. 6 + 5 = 11

____

Problem Solving

Write the number sentence. Solve.

7. 4 fly in the cave.

3 join them.

How many in all?

____ 

8. 3 are in a tree.

4 are in another tree.

Now how many are in trees?

____ 

Notes for Home Your child used turnaround facts to find sums to 12. *Home Activity:* Ask your child to tell you a set of turnaround facts with a sum of 8. (Possible answer: 5 + 3 = 8 and 3 + 5 = 8)

Name ____________________

Ways to Make Numbers

Use cubes. Show different ways to make 9.
Write the number sentences.

1.

Ways to Make 9	
0 + 9 = 9	___ + ___ = ___
___ + ___ = ___	___ + ___ = ___
___ + ___ = ___	___ + ___ = ___
___ + ___ = ___	___ + ___ = ___
___ + ___ = ___	___ + ___ = ___

Problem Solving Patterns

2. How many ways are there to make 7? ___

3. How many ways are there to make 8? ___

4. How many ways are there to make 9? ___

5. How many ways do you think there are to make 10? ___

6. How many ways do you think there are to make 11? ___

7. Why do you think so?

Notes for Home Your child found all the ways to make 9. *Home Activity:* Ask your child what pattern he or she can use to tell the number of ways to make 7, 6 or 5. (Possible answer: There is 1 more way than the sum; 8 ways to make 7, 7 ways to make 6, and 6 ways to make 5.)

Name ___________________________

Count Back and Subtract Zero

Practice 2-8

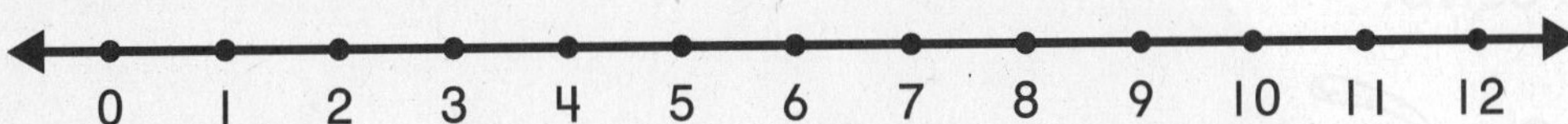

Use the number line. Write the difference.

1. 7 − 1 = 6 3 − 2 = 9 − 0 = 3 − 1 = 5 − 1 = 12 − 2 =

2. 3 − 0 = 11 − 2 = 6 − 1 = 2 − 2 = 1 − 0 = 9 − 1 =

3. 6 − 2 = 7 − 0 = 8 − 2 = 11 − 3 = 5 − 2 = 10 − 1 =

Mixed Practice

Add or subtract.

4. 9 − 2 = 8 + 2 = 5 − 0 = 7 − 2 = 1 + 8 = 4 + 2 =

Problem Solving Critical Thinking

Start with 8. Subtract a number.

The answer is 8. What did you subtract? _____

Notes for Home Your child added and subtracted using a number line. *Home Activity:* Ask your child to use the number line to find 8 + 3 = 11 and 9 - 2 = 7.

Name ______________________

Practice 2-9

Explore How Many More

Use ⬭ ⬬ to solve.

1. There are 12 🥄.

   There are 8 🔪.

   How many more 🥄 are there?

   4 more

2. There are 10 napkins.

   There are 8 cups.

   How many more napkins are there?

   ______ more

3. There are 9 plates.

   There are 5 bowls.

   How many more plates are there?

   ______ more

4. There are 12 🥄.

   There are 5 bowls.

   How many more 🥄 are there?

   ______ more

Problem Solving Visual Thinking

How many more plates than bowls?

______ more

How many mo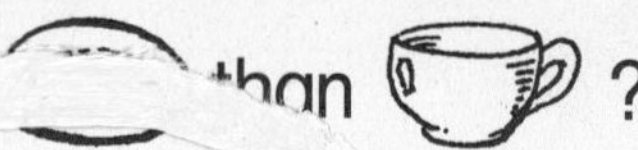than cups?

______ more

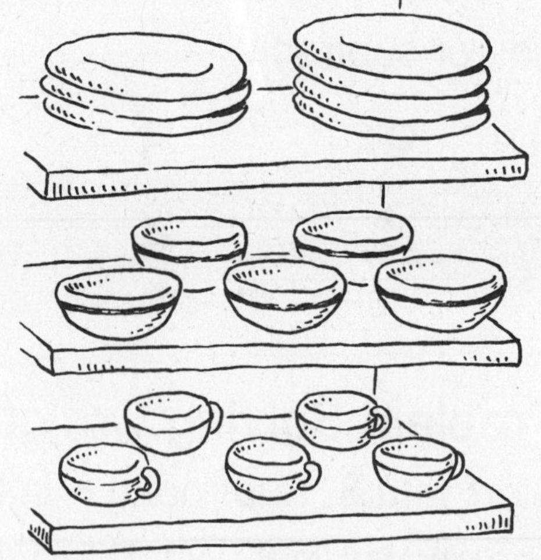

Note ~~r~~ **Home** Your child used counters to compare groups. *Home Activity:* Ask your child to take 3 cups and 5 sau[illegible] and compare the two groups. (There are 2 more saucers.)

Name ______________________________

Practice 2-10

Find How Many More

Write the number sentence. Solve.

You can use 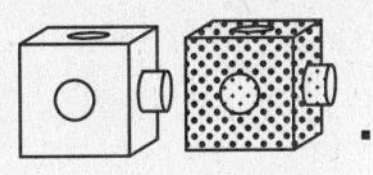 .

1. Lou eats 9 .

   Sue eats 5 .

   How many more does Lou eat than Sue?

   ____ − ____ = ____ more

2. Dan eats 8 .

   Nan eats 4 .

   How many more does Dan eat than Nan?

   ____ − ____ = ____ more

3. Mario sees 12 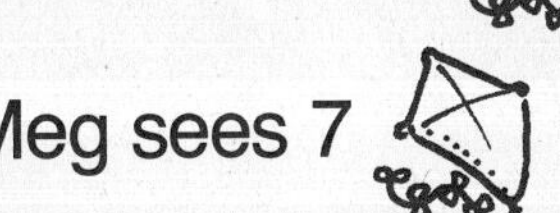 .

   Meg sees 7 .

   How many more did Mario see than Meg?

   ____ − ____ = ____ more

4. Anna sees 10 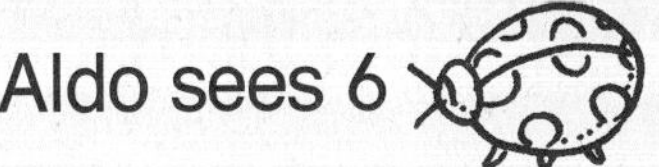 .

   Aldo sees 6 .

   How many more did Anna see than Aldo?

   ____ − ____ = ____ more

Problem Solving Visual Thinking

5. Draw less than 8 on the plate.

   How many more 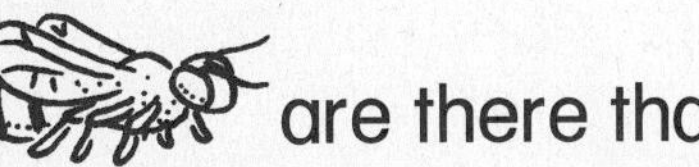 are there than ?

   ____ − ____ = ____ more

Notes for Home Your child used subtraction to compare groups. *Home Activity:* Show your child two groups of objects, such as 5 cups and 3 saucers. Have your child write a number sentence that tells how many more are in the larger group. (Possible answer: 5 – 3 = 2; there are 2 more cups.)

Name ______________________________

Relate Addition and Subtraction

Practice 2-11

Add or subtract.

Write the number sentence. Solve.

1. Kathy has 9 .

   Anne brings 5 more .

   How many  are there in all?

   ____ + ____ = ____

2. 14  are in a box.

   Anne took 5 .

   How many  were left?

   ____ − ____ = ____

3. 5  are on a leaf.

   7 more  join them.

   How many  are on the leaf now?

   ____ + ____ = ____

4. There are 12 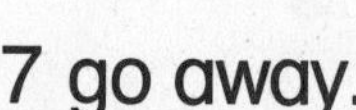 on a leaf.

   7 go away.

   How many are on the leaf now?

   ____ − ____ = ____

Tell a Math Story

Look at the picture. Tell stories to match the number sentences.

5. 4 + 3 = 7
6. 7 − 3 = 4

Notes for Home Your child chose addition or subtraction to solve word problems. *Home Activity:* Ask your child to tell you a story for the picture at the bottom of the page.

Name ______________________________

Practice 2-12

Problem Solving: Choose an Operation

Circle **add** or **subtract**.

Write the number sentence. Solve.

1. 6 are on a pond.

3 more  join them.

How many are on the pond now?

add **subtract**

 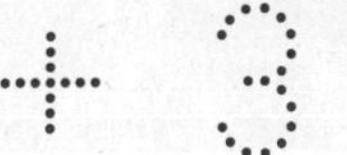

2. 3  play in a field.

1 runs away.

How many  are on the field now?

add **subtract**

____

3. There are 5 .

Pat drinks 2 .

How many  are there now?

add **subtract**

____

4. Jo cooks 7 .

Vi cooks 4 more .

How many cooked are there now?

add **subtract**

____

Write About It

5. Make up your own word problem.

Have a friend write a number sentence to solve it.

Notes for Home Your child practiced choosing addition or subtraction to solve problems. *Home Activity:* Ask your child to make up two problems, one that can be solved by adding and one that can be solved by subtracting.

Name ______________________________

Practice
Chapter 2
B

Mixed Practice: Lessons 7–12

Subtract. You can use .

1.

7	9	6	12	5	11	8
− 3	− 2	− 4	− 5	− 0	− 3	− 8

Problem Solving

Subtract. Write the number sentence.

2. 6 are on the bush.

   Martha cuts 5 .

   How many are left?

   ______________ 

3. 9  are in a bowl.

   Birds eat 5 .

   How many  are left?

   ____

Circle **add** or **subtract**. Write a number sentence.
Solve. You can use  .

4. 3 girls are walking.
   2 more girls join them.
   How many girls are walking now?

   add **subtract**

   ______________ girls

5. 8 boys are on seesaws.
   6 boys go home.
   How many boys are on the seesaw now?

   add **subtract**

   ______________ boys

Journal

6. Write your own word problem using the numbers 6, 6, and 12.
   Would you add or subtract to solve it? Write the number sentence.

Notes for Home Your child practiced subtraction and problem-solving skills. *Home Activity:* Ask your child to tell you a word problem that can be solved by adding.

Name ______________________________

Practice
Chapters 1–2
B

Cumulative Review

Write the number sentence. Solve.

1. 8 are playing.

3 run away.

How many are still playing?

____ − ____ = ____

2. 7 are in a box.

3 are outside.

How many are there in all?

____ + ____ = ____

Count back by ones. Write the numbers.

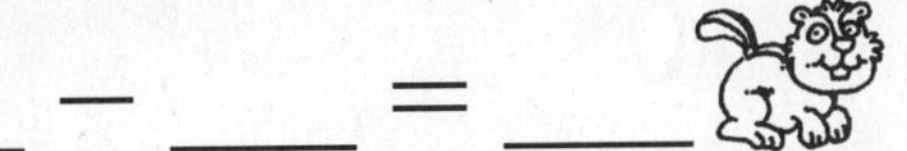

3. 36, 35, 34, ____, ____, ____, ____, ____, ____

Count by ones. Write the numbers.

4. 73, 74, 75, ____, ____, ____, ____, ____, ____

Test Prep

Fill in the ○ for the correct answer.

5. Which train and number sentence show the turnaround fact for this train and number sentence?

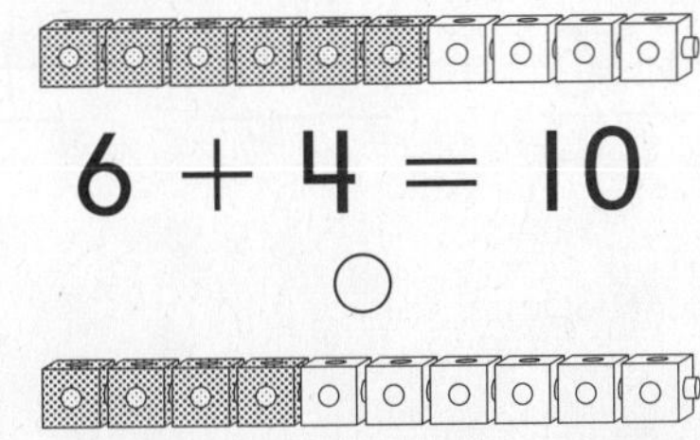

$6 + 4 = 10$

○ $5 + 5 = 10$

○ $4 + 6 = 10$

○ $7 + 3 = 10$

Notes for Home Your child reviewed addition and subtraction skills. *Home Activity:* Ask your child to tell what the turnaround fact for 7 + 3 = 10 would be. (3 + 7 = 10)

Name ______________________

Explore Doubles

Practice 3-1

5 + 5 = 10

Add. Write the sums. You can use [cubes].

1. 3 + 3 = ____ 6 + 6 = ____ 8 + 8 = ____

2. 7 + 7 = ____ 1 + 1 = ____ 4 + 4 = ____

3. 2 + 2 = ____ 9 + 9 = ____ 5 + 5 = ____

4.

7	6	5	4	3	2	1
+ 7	+ 6	+ 5	+ 4	+ 3	+ 2	+ 1

5.

3	7	6	4	9	4	8
+ 3	+ 7	+ 6	+ 4	+ 9	+ 4	+ 8

Talk About It

Look at Exercise 4. What pattern do you see in the sums?

Notes for Home Your child found the sums for doubles facts (such as 4 + 4 = 8). *Home Activity:* Ask your child to give one example of a doubles fact (3 + 3 = 6) and one example of an addition sentence that is not a doubles fact (3 + 5 = 8).

Name ______________________

Practice 3-2

Use Doubles Plus One

Add.

1. 5 + 5 = 10   5 + 6 = ____   6 + 5 = ____

2. 8 + 8 = ____   8 + 9 = ____   9 + 8 = ____

3. 6 + 6   6 + 7   7 + 6

4. 7 + 7   7 + 8   8 + 7

5. 2 + 2   5 + 5   1 + 1   9 + 9   6 + 6   7 + 7   4 + 4

6. 5 + 6   2 + 1   6 + 7   5 + 4   8 + 7   2 + 3   4 + 3

Mixed Practice Add.

7. 7 + 0   4 + 4   9 + 5   6 + 7   7 + 3   6 + 6   8 + 9

Problem Solving Critical Thinking

8. A [ladybug] has landed on a mirror. How many legs can you see? Explain your answer.

Notes for Home Your child solved addition facts with sums through 18. *Home Activity:* Ask your child how to solve 6 + 7. (6 + 6 = 12 plus 1 = 13)

Name ____________________

Practice 3-3

Explore Making 10

Put a picture in each empty box.
Complete the number sentence.

1. 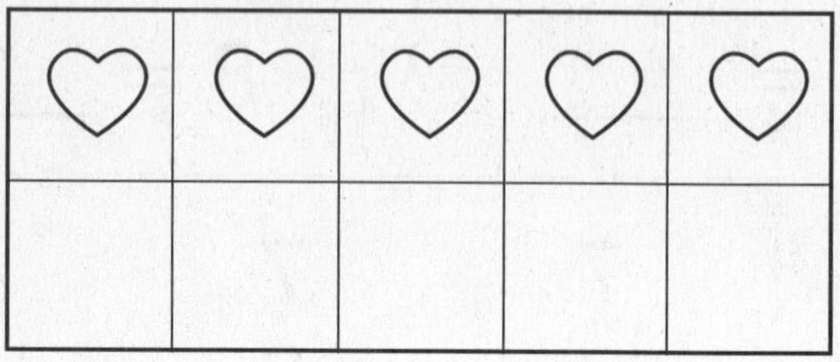 5 + ____ = ____

2.  3 + ____ = ____

3. 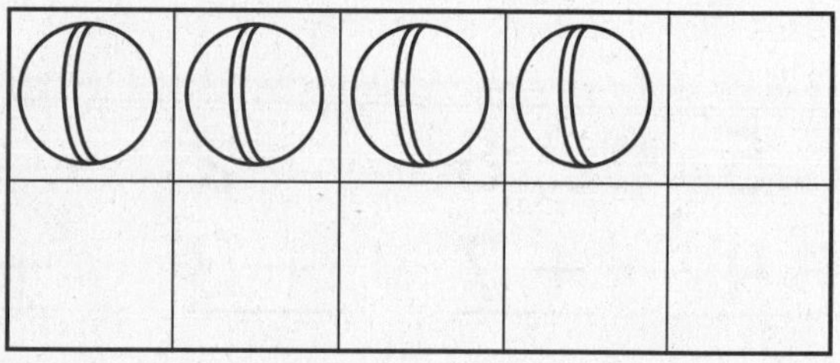 4 + ____ = ____

4. 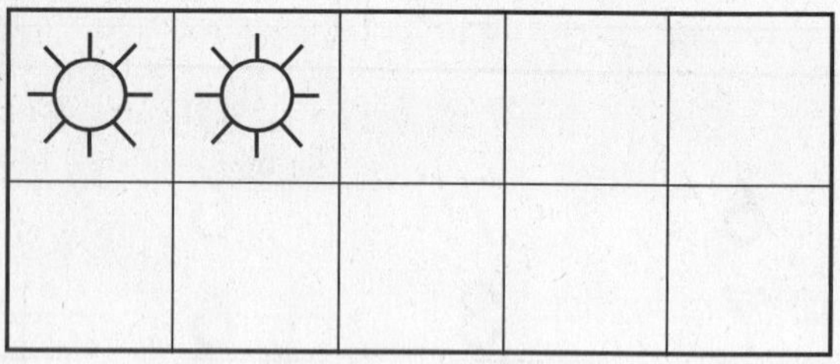 2 + ____ = ____

Talk About It What number would you add to 10 to make the sum of 10?

Notes for Home Your child drew pictures and wrote number sentences with the sum of 10. *Home Activity:* Ask your child to use objects to show 5 + 5 = 10 and to write the number sentence.

Name ______________________

Practice 3-4

Make 10 When Adding 9

Add. Write the addition sentence.

1. 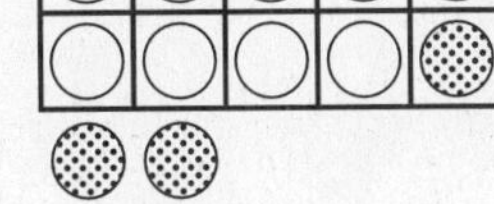

9 + 3 = 12

2. 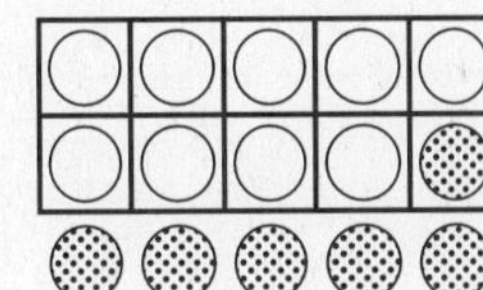

____ + ____ = ____

3. 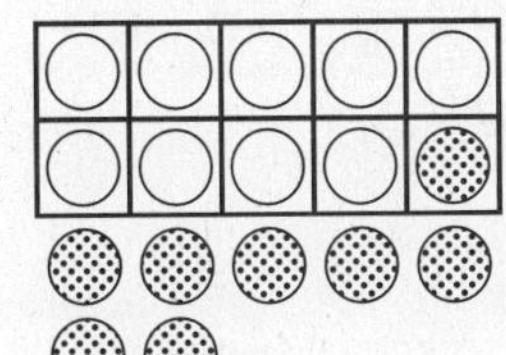

____ + ____ = ____

4. 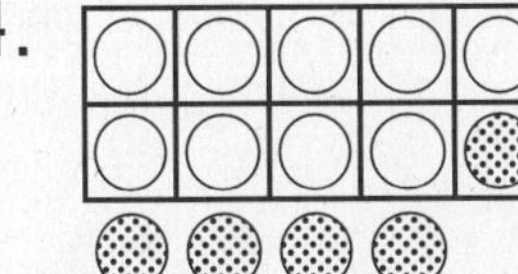

____ + ____ = ____

Add.

5.
$$\begin{array}{r} 9 \\ +5 \\ \hline \end{array} \quad \begin{array}{r} 9 \\ +8 \\ \hline \end{array} \quad \begin{array}{r} 9 \\ +2 \\ \hline \end{array} \quad \begin{array}{r} 9 \\ +7 \\ \hline \end{array} \quad \begin{array}{r} 9 \\ +3 \\ \hline \end{array} \quad \begin{array}{r} 9 \\ +6 \\ \hline \end{array} \quad \begin{array}{r} 9 \\ +4 \\ \hline \end{array}$$

Mixed Practice Add.

6. 5 + 4 = ____   7 + 7 = ____   9 + 8 = ____

Problem Solving Visual Thinking

Frank has 9 stamps on his card.

He gets 8 more stamps.

How many stamps does he have in all? ____ stamps

How many stamps will he carry over to a new card? ____ stamps

Notes for Home Your child practiced adding 9 to another number by first making a ten. *Home Activity:* Ask your child to explain how he or she solved Exercise 3.

Name ______________________________

Make 10 When Adding 6, 7, or 8

Practice 3-5

Add. Write the addition sentence.

1. 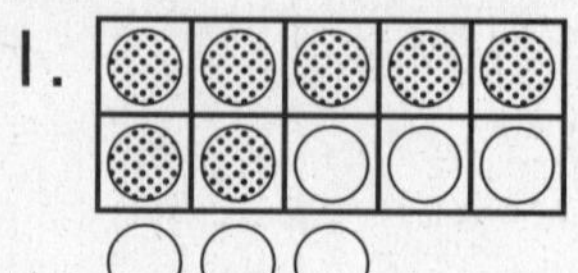

7 + 6 = 13

2. 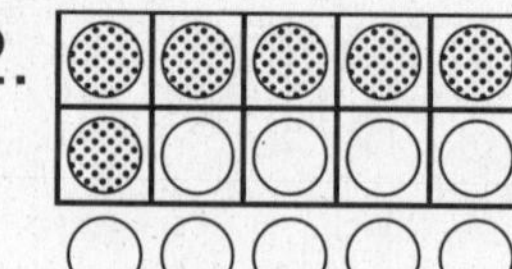

____ + ____ = ____

3. 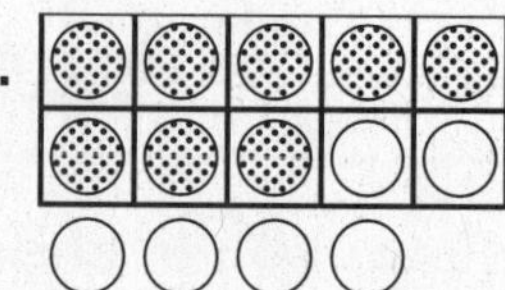

____ + ____ = ____

4. 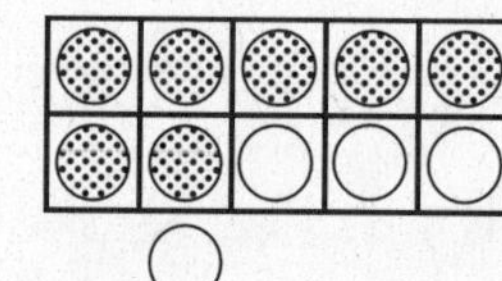

____ + ____ = ____

Add.

5.

6	4	7	8	9	8	5
+ 7	+ 7	+ 5	+ 5	+ 6	+ 8	+ 6

Problem Solving Critical Thinking

6. Maria tossed these numbers.

What is the sum? ____

7. Roberto tossed a sum of 13. Circle the cubes that he might have rolled.

7 8 5

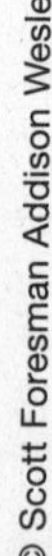

Notes for Home Your child practiced adding 6, 7, or 8 to another number by first making a ten. *Home Activity:* Ask your child to explain how he or she would find 7 + 5. (7 + 3 = 10 plus 2 = 12)

Name ______________________________

Practice 3-6

Problem Solving: Make a List

Martha has 15 special marbles.
Her father built 2 boxes for Martha to keep them.

Find all the ways Martha can put 15 marbles in 2 boxes.
You can use [cubes].
Write your numbers in the list.

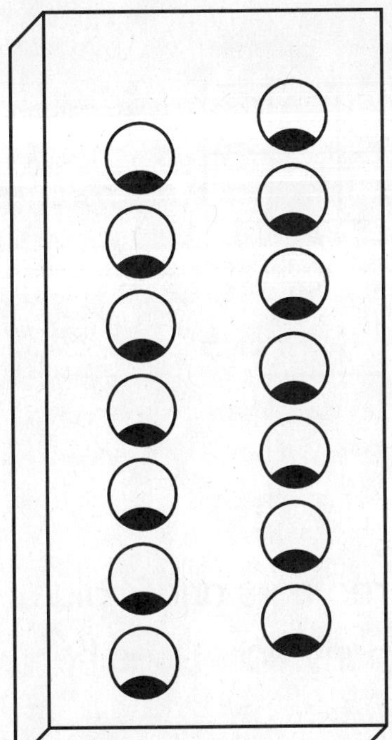
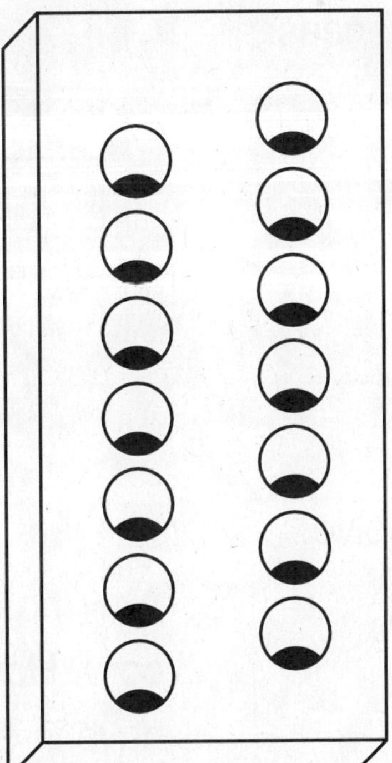

Left Box	Right Box
14	1
___	___
___	___
___	___
___	___
___	___
___	___
___	___
___	___
___	___
___	___
___	___
___	___
___	___

Patterns

What patterns do you see in your list?

Notes for Home Your child practiced making a list to solve a problem. *Home Activity:* Ask your child to make a list to show all the ways that 6 bananas can be put in 2 baskets. (1 and 5, 2 and 4, 3 and 3, 4 and 2, 5 and 1)

Name ______________________________

Practice
Chapter 3
A

Mixed Practice: Lessons 1–6

Add.

1. 6 + 6 = ____ 5 + 5 = ____ 4 + 4 = ____

Complete the number sentences.

2. 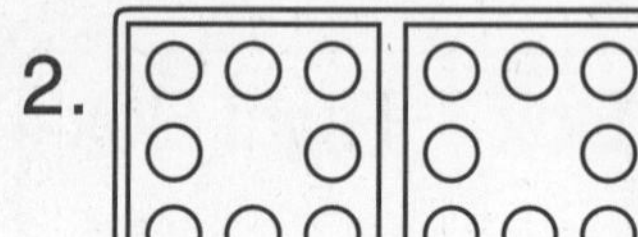 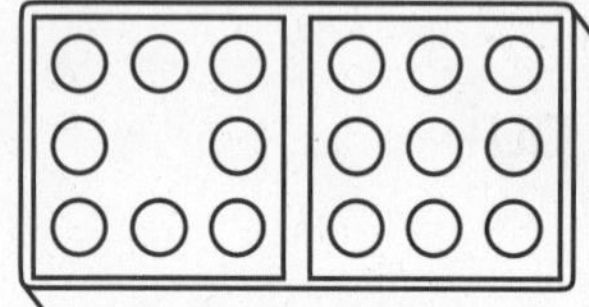 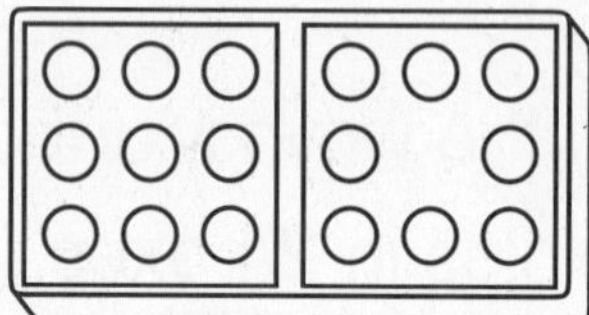

8 + 8 = ___ 8 + ___ = ___ 9 + ___ = ___

Add. Write the number sentences.

3. 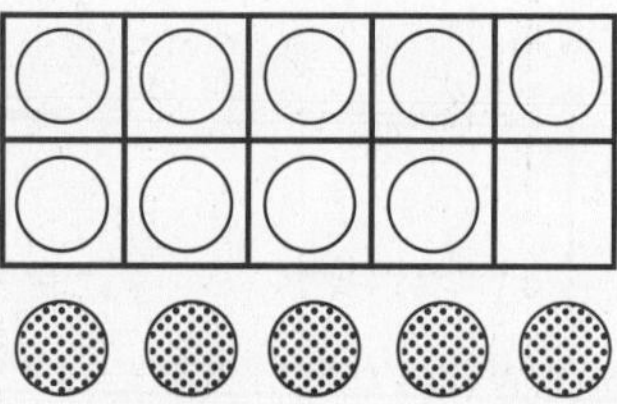

____ + ____ = ____

4. 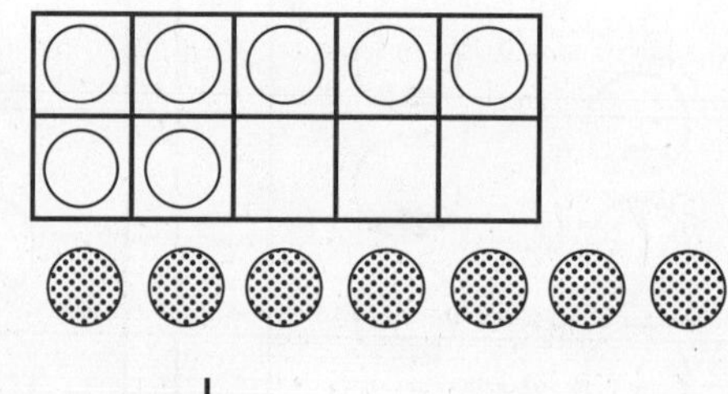

____ + ____ = ____

Problem Solving

Write a number sentence. Solve.

5. Mark's cat had 6 kittens. His dog had 5 puppies. How many puppies and kittens are there in all?

____ + ____ = ____

6. Amir has 8 red cars and 7 blue cars. How many cars does he have in all?

____ + ____ = ____

Journal

Draw a picture to show doubles plus one.

Notes for Home Your child practiced concepts, skills, and problem solving from Lessons 1 through 6.
Home Activity: Ask your child to use a 10-frame to show you how he or she would find the sum of 8 + 6. (14)

Name ______________________________

Practice
Chapters 1–3
A

Cumulative Review

Continue the pattern.
Write the missing numbers.

1. 2, 4, 6, _____, _____, _____

2. 4, 8, 12, _____, _____, _____

Add.

3. $\begin{array}{r} 6 \\ +8 \\ \hline \end{array}$ $\begin{array}{r} 9 \\ +3 \\ \hline \end{array}$ $\begin{array}{r} 4 \\ +7 \\ \hline \end{array}$

Problem Solving

Solve. Write a number sentence.

4. Stephanie had 6 stickers.
Suli gave her 7 more.
How many stickers does she have in all?

_____ + _____ = _____ stickers

Test Prep

Fill in the ○ to show the correct answer.

5. Which color do most children like best?

Brown ○ Yellow ○ Blue ○ Red ○

6. How many more children like blue than brown?

5 ○ 3 ○ 4 ○ 6 ○

Favorite Colors	
Brown	☺☺☺
Yellow	☺☺☺☺☺☺☺☺☺
Blue	☺☺☺☺☺☺☺
Red	☺☺☺☺☺

Notes for Home Your child reviewed number patterns, addition and subtraction facts to 12, and pictographs.
Home Activity: Ask your child explain how he or she determined the pattern in Exercise 2.

Name ______________________________

Practice 3-7

Use Doubles to Subtract

Add or subtract.

Match each doubles fact with a subtraction fact.

1. 8 − 4 = 4	8 + 8 = ____
2. 18 − 9 = ____	5 + 5 = ____
3. 16 − 8 = ____	9 + 9 = ____
4. 10 − 5 = ____	4 + 4 = 8

Subtract. Write the double that helps.

5. 12 − 6 = 6   6 + 6 = 12

6. 6 − 3 = ____   ____ + ____ = ____

7. 14 − 7 = ____   ____ + ____ = ____

Mental Math

Felix and Dina have shell collections. Both collections have two kinds of shells which are equal in number. Write the number of shells each child has.

8. Felix has 16 shells.

____ are pink shells.

____ are white shells.

9. Dina has 14 shells.

____ are conch shells.

____ are snail shells.

Notes for Home Your child matched addition and subtraction facts. *Home Activity:* Ask your child what doubles fact helps to find 12 − 6. (6 + 6 = 12)

Name ______________________

Practice 3-8

Use Addition Facts to Subtract

Add or subtract. Color each addition fact to match the related subtraction fact. Use a different color for each set of facts.

1.

11 − 5	16 − 8	13 − 9	9 − 6
18 − 9	12 − 7	14 − 6	15 − 8

2.

8 + 8	3 + 6	9 + 9	5 + 7
4 + 9	7 + 8	6 + 5	8 + 6

Tell a Math Story

3. Tell an addition story and a related subtraction story for the picture.

Notes for Home Your child used addition facts to subtract. *Home Activity:* Ask your child to explain how 4 + 8 = 12 helps to find 12 − 8 = 4.

Name ________________________________

Practice 3-9

Relate Addition and Subtraction

Write a number sentence. Solve.

1. Stacy had 5 celery sticks on her plate.She gave 3 to her brother. How many were left?

   ____

2. There were 2 carrot sticks on Stacy's plate. Her brother gave her 3 of his carrot sticks. How many carrot sticks does Stacy have?

   ____

Write About It

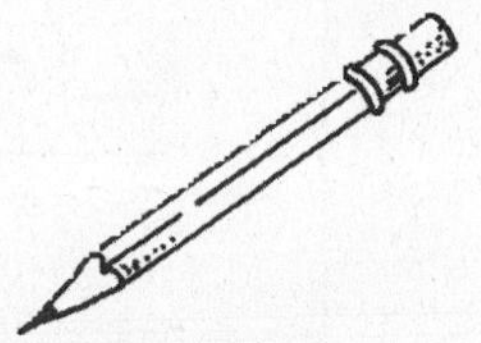

3. Use the numbers 8, 9, and 17.
   Write an addition story and a related subtraction story.

Write number sentences for your stories.

____________________ ____________________

Notes for Home Your child practiced writing and solving story problems with related facts. *Home Activity:* Ask your child to write related addition and subtraction facts using these numbers: 9, 4, 13. (9 + 4 = 13 or 4 + 9 = 13 and 13 – 4 = 9 or 13 - 9 = 4)

Name ______________________________

Practice 3-10

Problem Solving: Group Decision Making

Work with a group to make a bar graph.

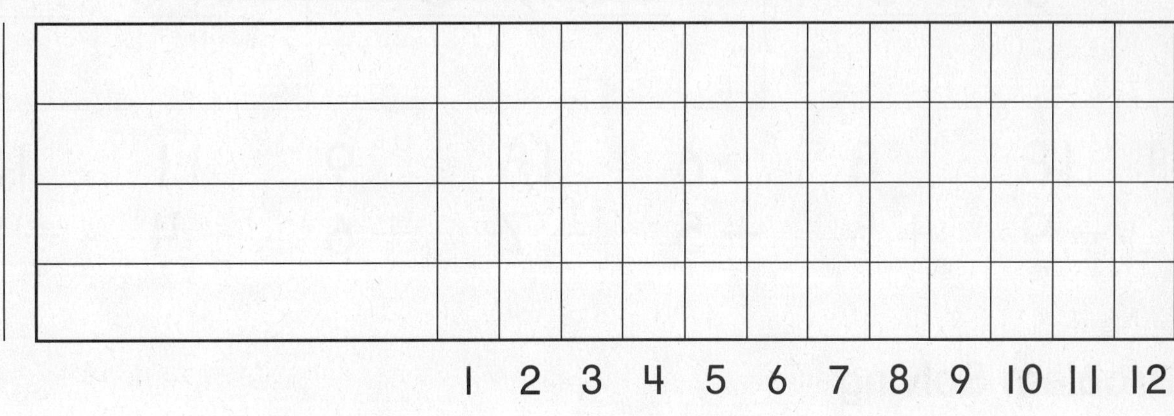

1. Write the title of your graph at the top.

2. Put a choice at the start of each row.

3. Label the side and bottom of your graph.

4. Color to show how many votes for each choice.

Write your own. With your group, decide on 2 questions that can be answered by your graph. Write your questions.

5. ______________________________

6. ______________________________

Journal

7. What did you learn about working in a group? What will you do the same way the next time? What might you change? Why?

Notes for Home Your child made a bar graph. *Home Activity:* Ask your child to describe how he or she worked with a group to collect the information and to create the graph.

Name ________________________________

Mixed Practice: Lessons 7–10

Add or subtract.

1.		2.		3.	
$8 + 8 =$	$16 - 8 =$	$9 + 8 =$	$17 - 8 =$	$8 + 6 =$	$14 - 6 =$

4.

$18 - 9 =$	$8 + 5 =$	$6 + 5 =$	$15 - 7 =$	$9 + 6 =$	$11 - 4 =$	$12 - 8 =$

Problem Solving

Write a number sentence. Solve.

5. Steven had 8 pennies.
He found 7 more.
How many does he have now?

____________________ pennies

6. Steven had 15 pennies.
He gave 7 to his sister.
How many does he have left?

____________________ pennies

Use the graph to answer the questions.

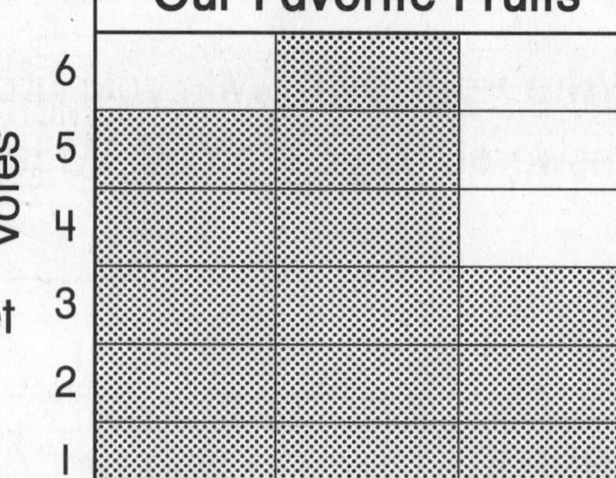

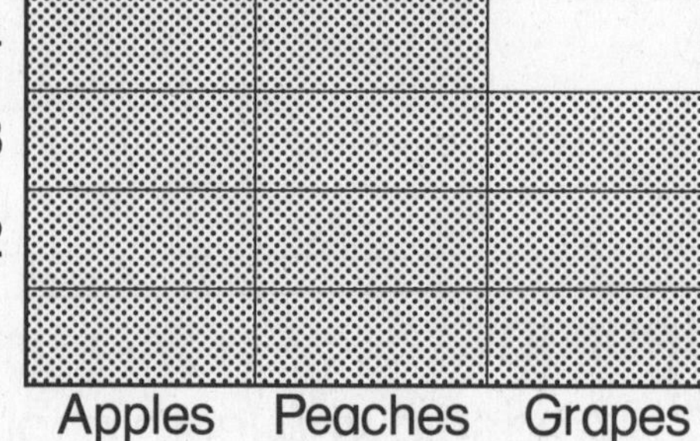

7. Which fruit got the most votes?

____

8. How many more votes did Apples get than Grapes? _____ more votes

Journal

9. Draw a picture to show these related facts:

$$8 + 6 = 14 \qquad 14 - 6 = 8$$

Notes for Home Your child practiced adding and subtracting related facts, reading a graph, and solving problems. *Home Activity:* Ask your child to tell you a related subtraction fact for 8 + 4 = 12 (12 – 4 = 8 or 12 – 8 = 4).

Name ____________________

Practice
Chapters 1–3
B

Cumulative Review

Write the number sentence. Then write the turnaround fact.

1.

____

____

2. 

____

____

Problem Solving

Write a number sentence. Solve.

3. Markus has 6 toy trucks
Marcy brings 6 more.
How many do they have in all?

____________ toy trucks

4. Marcy brings 7 toy trucks.
Markus still has 6.
How many do they have now?

____________ toy trucks

Test Prep

Fill in the ○ for the correct answer.
What fact matches each picture?

5.

12 − 4 ○ 7 + 4 ○ 7 + 5 ○ 7 − 5 ○

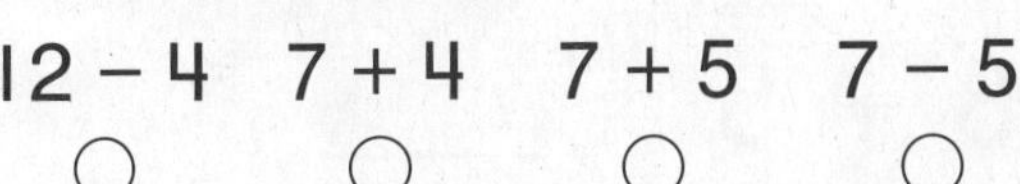

6. 

13 − 9 ○ 9 + 4 ○ 13 + 4 ○ 9 − 4 ○

Notes for Home Your child reviewed addition and subtraction facts to 12. *Home Activity:* Ask your child to tell you the turnaround fact for 2 + 9. (9 + 2 = 11)

Name ____________________________

Practice 4-1

Explore Fact Families

5 + 9 = 14

14 − 5 = 9

9 + 5 = 14

14 − 9 = 5

Complete each fact family.
Add or subtract.

1.

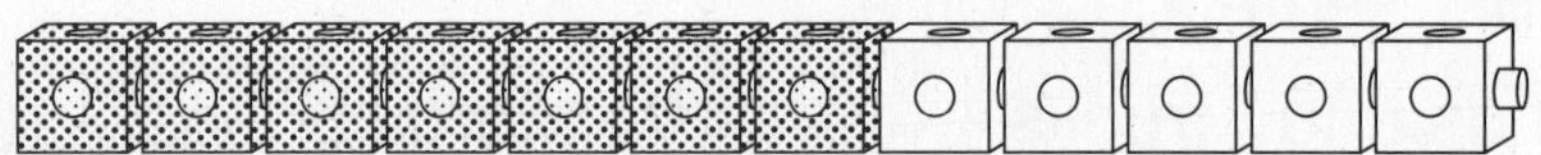

7 + 5 = ____

12 − 7 = ____

5 + 7 = ____

12 − 5 = ____

2.

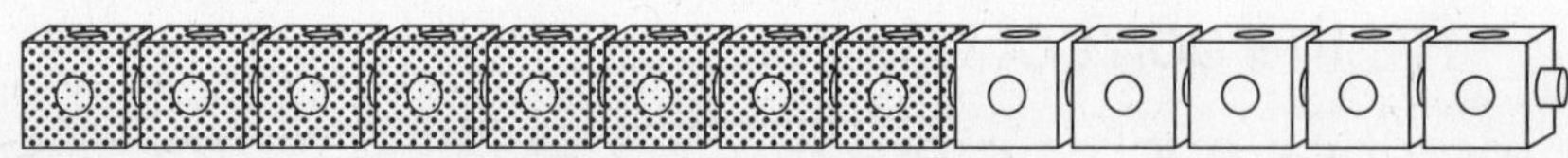

8 + 5 = ____

13 − 5 = ____

5 + 8 = ____

13 − 8 = ____

Talk About It

Tell the fact family for the numbers 8, 6, and 14.

Notes for Home Your child added and subtracted using fact families. *Home Activity:* Ask your child to write the fact family for the numbers 6, 6, and 12. (6 + 6 = 12; 12 - 6 = 6)

Name ______________________

Practice 4-2

Fact Families

Complete each fact family. Add or subtract

1. $4 + 9 =$ ____
   $9 + 4 =$ ____
   $13 - 9 =$ ____
   $13 - 4 =$ ____

2. $7 + 9 =$ ____
   $9 + 7 =$ ____
   $16 - 9 =$ ____
   $16 - 7 =$ ____

3. $8 + 9 =$ ____
   $9 + 8 =$ ____
   $17 - 9 =$ ____
   $17 - 8 =$ ____

4. $9 + 6 =$ ____
   $6 + 9 =$ ____
   $15 - 6 =$ ____
   $15 - 9 =$ ____

5. $\begin{array}{r} 8 \\ +8 \\ \hline \end{array}$ $\begin{array}{r} 16 \\ -8 \\ \hline \end{array}$

6. $\begin{array}{r} 6 \\ +6 \\ \hline \end{array}$ $\begin{array}{r} 12 \\ -6 \\ \hline \end{array}$

Problem Solving Critical Thinking

Write two different fact families using the number 11.

Notes for Home Your child added and subtracted using fact families. *Home Activity:* Ask your child to explain why he or she can write only two number facts using 6 and 12. (Possible answer: A fact family with doubles has only 2 facts; others have four.)

Name ______________________________

Practice 4-3

Use Addition to Check Subtraction

Use these numbers. Write a subtraction fact.

Write an addition fact to check.

1\. 14 6

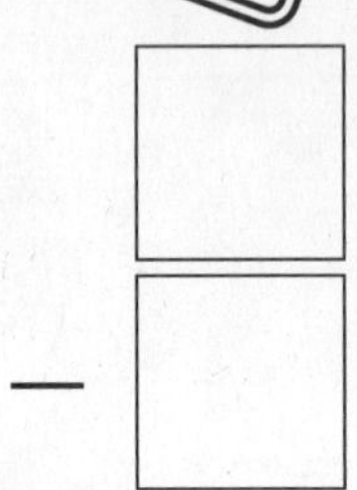
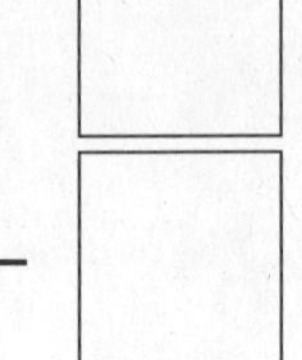

□ □
− □ + □
___ ___

2\. 17 8

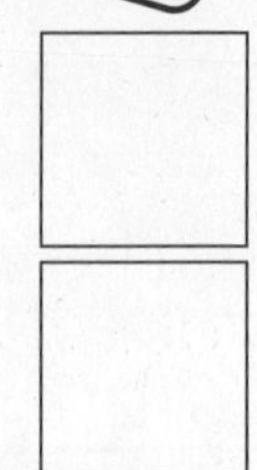

□ □
− □ + □
___ ___

3\. 15 9

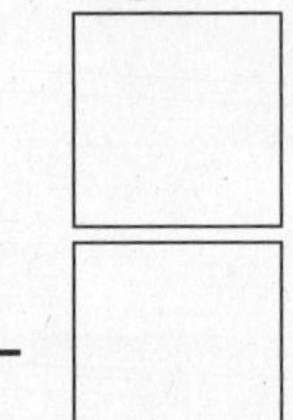
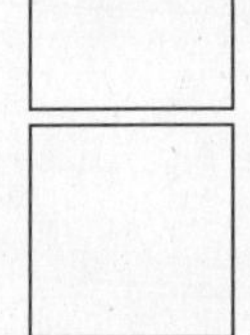

□ □
− □ + □
___ ___

4\. 13 6

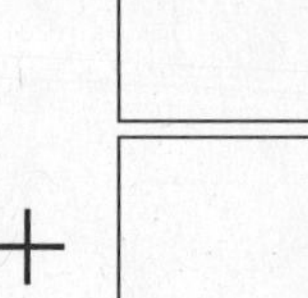

□ □
− □ + □
___ ___

5\. 16 7

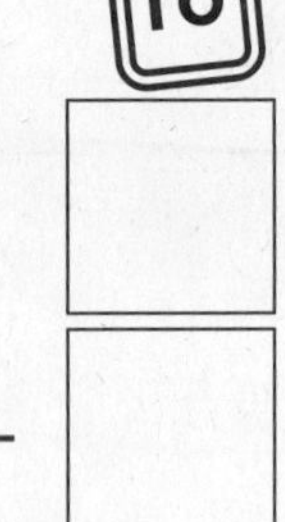
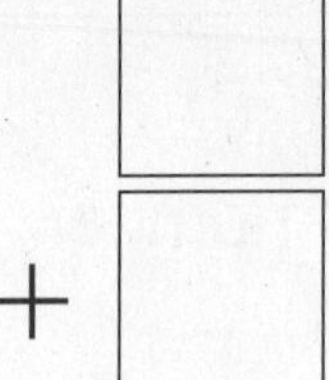

□ □
− □ + □
___ ___

6\. 13 8

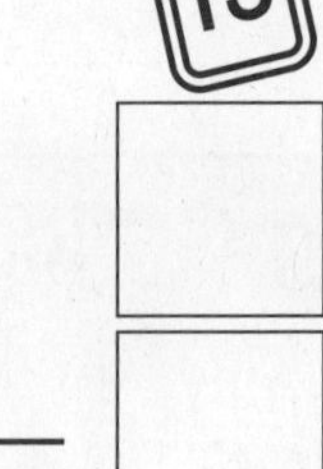
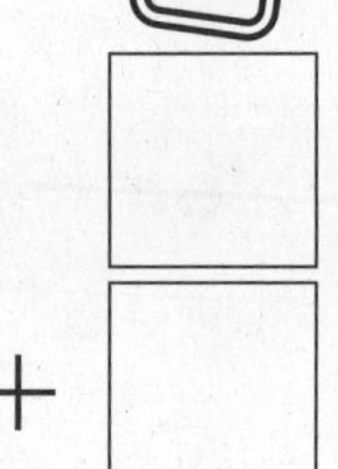

□ □
− □ + □
___ ___

Problem Solving

Complete the number sentence. 15 − 7= _____

Write two related addition facts that you can use to check your answer.

Notes for Home Your child checked subtraction problems using addition. *Home Activity:* Ask your child to subtract 14 − 8 and to check the answer by adding. (14 − 8 = 6; 8 + 6 = 14)

Name ______________________

Practice 4-4

Problem Solving: Draw a Picture

Draw a picture to solve the problem.

1. Tia made 8 muffins. She ate 1 muffin and Sara ate 2 muffins. They each ate 1 muffin later. How many muffins were left?

   ______ muffins

Write About It

2. Write another problem. Ask a friend to draw a picture to solve it.

   ____

   ____

   ____

   ____

   ____

Notes for Home Your child drew pictures to solve problems. *Home Activity:* Have your child draw pictures to solve this word problem: There were four apples in the bowl. Jim took one to school for lunch. His mother had one. His brother ate two more. How many apples were left? (No apples were left.)

Name ______________________

Practice
Chapter 4
A

Mixed Practice: Lessons 1–4

Write the number sentences to make a fact family.

1. (cubes: 8 shaded, 6 white)

____ + ____ = ____   ____ – ____ = ____

____ + ____ = ____   ____ – ____ = ____

Subtract. Then write a related addition fact.

2. 14 – 9 = ____   ____ + ____ = ____

3. 13 – 5 = ____   ____ + ____ = ____

Problem Solving

Draw a picture to solve the problem.

4. Kim blew 16 bubbles.
His brother broke 5.
3 more flew away.
How many were left?

____ bubbles

Journal

5. Write a problem about a picnic. Draw a picture.
Write the fact family that your picture shows.

Notes for Home Your child practiced addition and subtraction facts and solving problems. *Home Activity:* Ask your child to write a related addition fact for 16 – 8 = 8. (8 + 8 = 16)

Name ____________________

Cumulative Review

Add.

1.

8	7	6	9	8	9	7
+ 5	+ 6	+ 9	+ 7	+ 7	+ 9	+ 5

Problem Solving

Use the graph to answer the questions.

2. How many children like plain popcorn?

   ______ children

3. How many more children like plain popcorn than butter popcorn?

   ______ more children

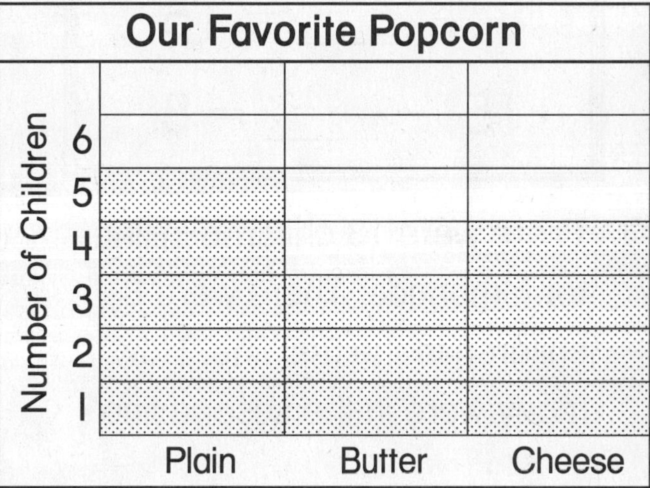

Test Prep

Fill in the ○ for the correct answer.

Solve each problem.

4. Roy has 8 green balls and 9 red balls. How many balls does he have?

   16 ○ 5 ○ 18 ○ 17 ○

5. Mr. Brown's class has 18 books. 9 are math books. How many are science books?

   6 ○ 9 ○ 8 ○ 7 ○

Notes for Home Your child reviewed addition facts, reading a graph, and solving word problems.
Home Activity: Ask your child how many fewer children like butter popcorn than cheese popcorn on the graph? (1)

Name ______________________

Practice 4-5

Missing Addends

Find the missing number.
Use the fact family to help you.

1\.

15 / 8

15 − 8 = ____

____ + 8 = ____

8 + ____ = 15

15 − ____ = 8

2\.

17 / 9

____ + 9 = 17

17 − 9 = ____

9 + ____ = 17

17 − ____ = 9

3\. There were 13 children in line for lemonade. There were 8 children in the first line. How many were in the second line?

____ children

4\. Ben had 5 kiddie car rides the first day. He rode 9 times the second day. How many rides did he have in all?

____ rides

Problem Solving Patterns

5\. Find the missing numbers. Find the pattern.
Write the next fact.

7	7	7	7	☐
+ ☐	+ ☐	+ ☐	+ ☐	+ ☐
8	10	12	14	☐

Notes for Home Your child used fact families to find missing numbers. *Home Activity:* Ask your child to solve 9 + __ = 15. (6)

Name ______________________________

Practice 4-6

Three Addends

Add across.

$5 + 4 + 6 = 15$

Add down.

$$\begin{array}{r} 4 \\ 7 \\ +\,2 \\ \hline 13 \end{array}$$

1.

2	1	5	
4	7	0	
6	3	5	

2.

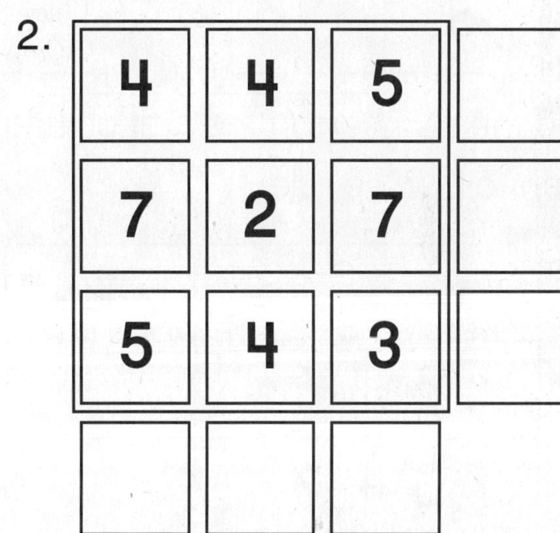

4	4	5	
7	2	7	
5	4	3	

Problem Solving

3. A team needs 10 points to win a prize. Find each team's total score. Circle the names of the winning teams.

Team	First Race	Second Race	Third Race	Total Score
Cats	8	0	1	_____ points
Stars	6	2	4	_____ points
Foxes	7	4	3	_____ points
Bears	1	5	5	_____ points

Notes for Home Your child added three numbers. *Home Activity:* Ask your child which team in the Problem Solving chart won the most points. (Foxes)

Name ______________________________

Use Addition and Subtraction Rules

Practice 4-7

Follow the rule. Add or subtract.

1.

Add 7	
7	
6	
9	

2.

Subtract 4	
12	
17	
13	

3.

Subtract 6	
14	
11	
15	

Add the numbers in the first column.
Then follow the rule.

4.

	Add 4
5 + 6	
3 + 7	
2 + 6	

5.

	Add 6
4 + 5	
6 + 5	
3 + 1	

Problem Solving

Write your own rule for each chart.
Then follow the rule. Add or subtract.

6.

Add ____	
5	
7	
8	

7.

Subtract ____	
18	
11	
13	

8.

Subtract ____	
14	
12	
15	

Notes for Home Your child added and subtracted. *Home Activity:* Ask your child to choose three numbers less than 10 and add 3 to each of them.

Name ______________________________

Practice 4-8

What's My Rule?

Find the rule. Then write the missing number.

1.

10	7
5	2
7	4
4	

2.

2 + 5	12
3 + 5	13
4 + 6	15
7 + 5	

Write you own tables.

Fill in the numbers. Ask a friend to find the rule.

3.

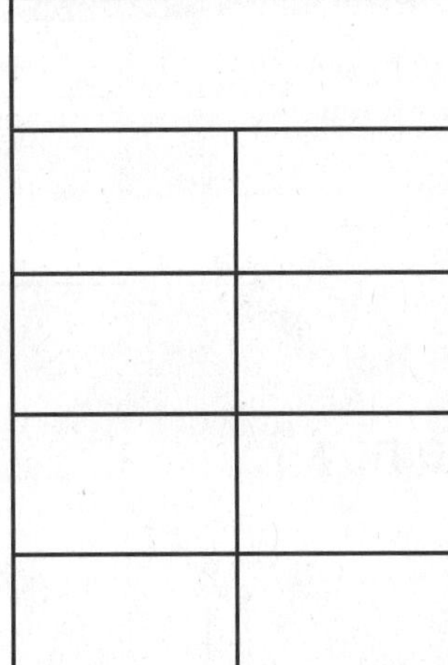

4.

Problem Solving

5. Shane made 6 key chains. Luis make 3 key chains. Rona made 5 key chains. They each sold 1 key chain at the class fair. How many key chains does each have now?

Shane: ______ key chains

Luis: ______ key chains

Rona: ______ key chains

Notes for Home Your child found the rule (such as add 3 or subtract 5) for addition and subtraction tables. *Home Activity:* Ask your child to explain his or her reasoning for solving the Problem Solving exercises.

Name ____________________

Problem Solving:
Multiple-Step Problems

Use .

Write each number sentence. Solve.

1. At the beach, Sam found 12 seashells. He lost 7. $12 - 7 = 5$ seashells

   Later, he found 6 more shells. How many does he have now? ________ seashells

2. Jamal bought 15 stickers. He used 7. ________ stickers

   He used 5 more. How many stickers does Jamal have now? ________ stickers

3. On the beach, Ali found 10 pennies. He spent 5. ________ pennies

   He spent 5 more. How many pennies does he have now? ________ pennies

Tell a Math Story

4. Tell a story problem about balloons. Include addition and subtraction in your story. Ask a friend to solve your problem.

Notes for Home Your child practiced solving word problems. *Home Activity:* Ask your child to tell you the word problem he or she made up for *Tell a Math Story*.

Name ______________________________

Practice
Chapter 4
B

Mixed Practice: Lessons 5–9

Find the missing number in the facts family.

1. $8 + \_\_\_ = 15$

$\_\_\_ + 8 = 15$

$15 - 8 = \_\_\_$

$15 - \_\_\_ = 8$

Add.

2.

$$\begin{array}{r} 8 \\ 1 \\ +\,2 \\ \hline \end{array} \qquad \begin{array}{r} 6 \\ 3 \\ +\,6 \\ \hline \end{array} \qquad \begin{array}{r} 7 \\ 3 \\ +\,5 \\ \hline \end{array}$$

Follow the rule.
Write the missing numbers.

3.

Add 7	
5	
4	

Find the rule.
Write the rule.

4.

17	9
14	6

Problem Solving

Write each number sentence. Solve.

5. Bob bought 9 plums.
He gave 2 to Sally. ______ plums

He bought 3 more plums.
How many plums does Bob have now? ______ plums

Journal

6. Write all the ways you can solve $6 + 4 + 5$.

Notes for Home Children practiced finding missing numbers, adding three numbers, and solving problems.
Home Activity: Ask your child to tell you how to find the missing numbers in Exercise 5.

Name ______________________

Cumulative Review

Add.

Write the number sentence.

1. 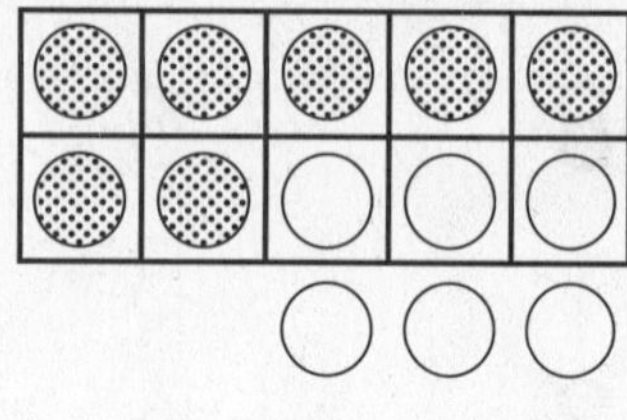

____ + ____ = ____

2. 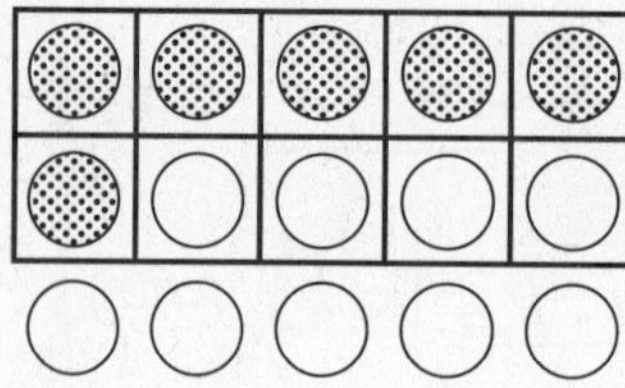

____ + ____ = ____

Problem Solving

Use the graph to answer the questions.

3. How many children had pony rides on Friday?

____ children

4. On which day did the most children take pony rides?

____

Number of Children on Pony Rides	
Friday	🧍 🧍 🧍 🧍
Saturday	🧍 🧍 🧍 🧍 🧍 🧍 🧍
Sunday	🧍 🧍 🧍 🧍 🧍 🧍

Each 🧍 stands for 10 children.

Test Prep

Fill in the ○ for the correct answer.

5. Which fact is shown in the picture.

3 + 5 ○ 4 + 4 ○ 5 + 4 ○ 5 + 5 ○

6. Add 7 more. How many in all?

13 ○
14 ○
15 ○

Notes for Home Your child reviewed numbers, used graphs to solve problems, and practiced addition facts. *Home Activity:* Ask your child to use the graph on this page to find how many children had pony rides on Sunday.

Name ______________________

Explore Estimation

Practice 5-1

tens	ones

tens	ones
1 ten	5 ones

Estimate. Try to take 10 .

Use your tens/ones mat. Make tens and ones.

Write how many tens and ones.

	Try to take this many.	Write how many.
1.	30	______ tens ______ ones
2.	40	______ tens ______ ones
3.	50	______ tens ______ ones
4.	60	______ tens ______ ones
5.	70	______ tens ______ ones
6.	80	______ tens ______ ones
7.	90	______ tens ______ ones

Talk About It Which time did you get the closest to your estimate? How close did you get? Tell a classmate.

Notes for Home Your child used grouping by tens to estimate and count. *Home Activity:* Put some macaroni or dried beans in 3 piles. Ask your child to divided each pile into groups of tens and ones, and to count how many there are in each pile.

Name ______________________

Practice 5-2

Record Numbers

Write how many tens and ones. Write the number.

1. 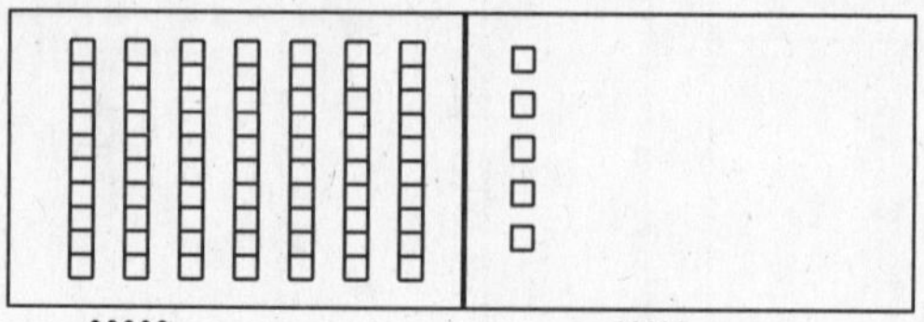 7 tens 5 ones

75

2. 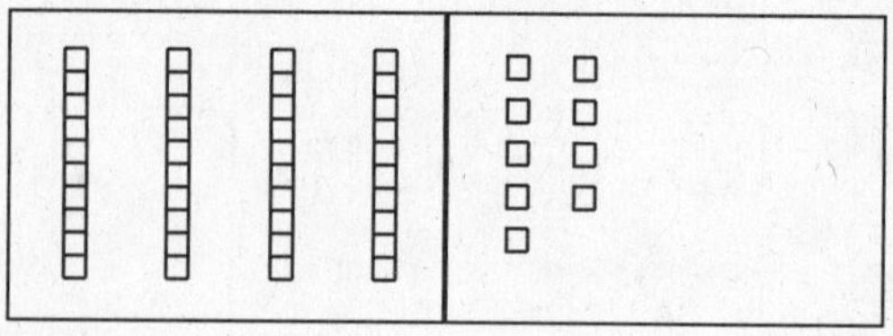 ______ tens ______ ones

______

Write the number.

3. 1 ten 4 ones

14

4. 6 tens 3 ones

______

5. 2 tens 5 ones

______

6. 8 tens 0 ones

______

7. 5 tens 0 ones

______

8. 0 tens 7 ones

______

9. 9 tens 6 ones

______

10. 6 tens 9 ones

______

Problem Solving Critical Thinking

11. Look at the numbers you wrote for Exercises 9 and 10. How are the numbers alike? How are they different?

Notes for Home Your child wrote numbers as tens and ones and as 2-digit numbers. *Home Activity:* Tell your child a number such as 4 tens and 6 ones and ask him or her to tell you the 2-digit number. (46.)

Name ____________________

Practice 5-3

Number Words

Write the number.

1. thirty-seven 37
2. fifty-six ______
3. eighty ______
4. seventy-one ______
5. Use the clues to write each word. Fill in the puzzle.

Across	Down
1. 28	2. 2
7. 1	3. 17
8. 5	4. 80
9. 20	5. 90
10. 10	6. 30
11. 70	8. 40
13. 60	11. 6
14. 4	12. 2

Problem Solving Critical Thinking

6. Pick a number that is greater than 10 and less than 100. What are some ways to show the number?

____

Notes for Home Your child practiced writing number words. *Home Activity:* Have your child think of a number between 40 and 60 and write the numeral and word for it. (Possible answer: 52, fifty-two)

Name ______________________

Practice 5-4

Tell About 100

These show 100.

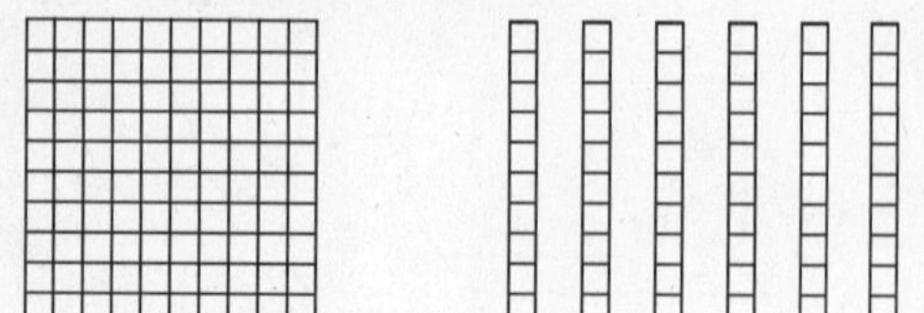

1. Color 70 red.
   Color 30 blue.
   Write how many.

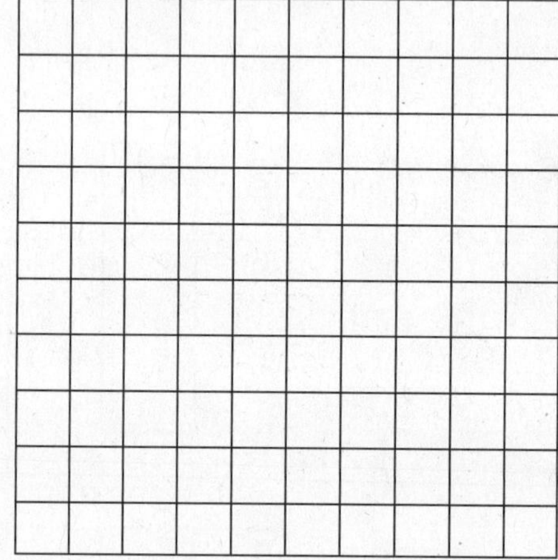

70 and 30 is 100.

Write your own.

2. Color some tens yellow.
   Color the rest of the tens green.
   Write how many.

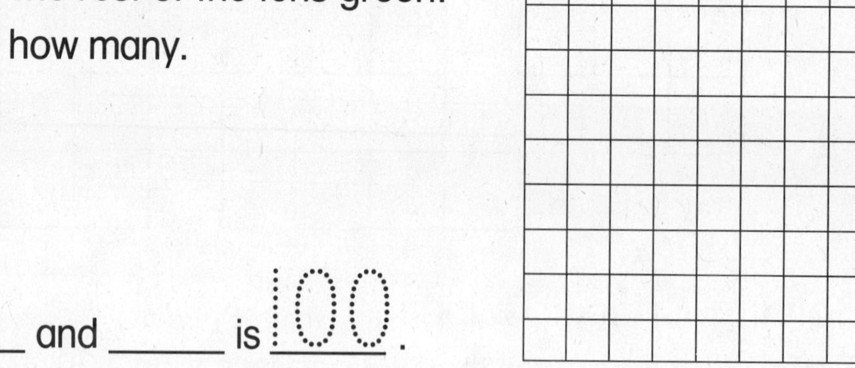

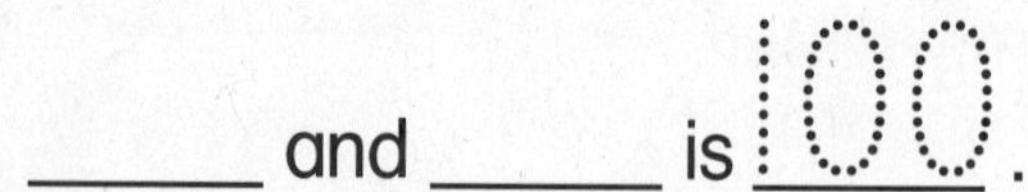

_____ and _____ is 100.

Problem Solving Critical Thinking

3. How could you use 4 colors to show 100?

Notes for Home Your child used a grid to show combinations of numbers that make 100. *Home Activity:* Tell your child 3 different numbers less than 100. Ask your child to tell you the numbers, that when added to each, would make 100.

Name ________________________

Practice 5-5

Problem Solving: Use Data from a Graph

Coin Collections	
Abe	○○○○○○
Beth	○○○○
Carlos	○○
Dory	○○○○○○○

Each ○ means 2 coins.

Use the graph to solve.

1. How many coins did Abe collect?

   12 coins

2. How many coins did Carlos collect?

   _____ coins

3. How many coins did Beth and Dory collect in all?

   _____ coins

4. How many more coins did Dory collect than Abe?

   _____ more

Visual Thinking

5. Carlos adds 14 more coins to his collection. What would you add to the graph? Explain.

Notes for Home Your child used a graph to answer questions. *Home Activity:* Ask your child to show you how to use the graph to count the coins in Dory's collection. (Possible answer: Each picture stands for 2. Count by 2s: 2, 4, 6, 8, 10, 12, 14.)

Name ______________________

Practice
Chapter 5
A

Mixed Practice: Lessons 1–5

Write how many tens and ones.
Write the number.

1.

tens	ones
▯▯▯▯▯▯	▫▫▫

_____ tens _____ ones

_____

Write the number.

2. twenty-seven _____

3. seventy-three _____

4. sixty-nine

5. forty-two

Problem Solving

Use the graph to answer the questions.

6. How many more books does Larry have than Leon?

_____ more

7. How many books do Leon and Lacy have together?

_____ books

Book Collections	
Larry	📖📖📖📖
Leon	📖📖📖
Lacy	📖📖📖📖📖📖📖📖

Each 📖 means 5 books

Journal

8. Pick an even and an odd number between 10 and 100. Draw pictures of tens and ones to show your numbers.

Notes for Home Your child counted by tens and ones, wrote numbers, and read graphs. *Home Activity:* Write the words for 3 numbers below 100. Ask your child to read the words aloud and to write the numbers. (Sample: twenty-two: 22; fifteen: 15; ninety-seven: 97)

 Use with page 167.

Name ______________________________

Practice
Chapters 1–5
A

Cumulative Review

Add or subtract.

1.

7	15	5	10	14	4	13
+ 5	− 6	+ 8	− 4	− 6	− 1	− 6

2.

6	15	9	11	8	5	10
+ 7	− 8	+ 9	− 3	+ 0	+ 6	− 2

Problem Solving

Solve.

3. Tia has 6 seashells.
Then she finds 4 more.
How many seashells does
Tia have now?

______ seashells

4. Tom has 9 seashells.
He gives 3 to Tia.
How many seashells does
Tom have now?

______ seashells

Test Prep

Fill in the ○ for the correct answer.

5. 7 + 2 + 6 = _____

○ 10 ○ 9 ○ 15 ○ 8

6. 4 + 3 + 7 = _____

○ 16 ○ 7 ○ 10 ○ 14

Notes for Home Your child reviewed addition and subtraction facts and problem solving. *Home Activity:* Ask your child how many tens and ones are in the number 85. (8 tens and 5 ones)

Name ________________________________

Practice
5-6

Hundred Chart and Skip Counting Patterns

1	2	3	4	5	6	7	8	9	10
11	12	13	14	15	16	17	18	19	20
21	22	23	24	25	26	27	28	29	30
31	32	33	34	35	36	37	38	39	40
41	42	43	44	45	46	47	48	49	50
51	52	53	54	55	56	57	58	59	60
61	62	63	64	65	66	67	68	69	70
71	72	73	74	75	76	77	78	79	80
81	82	83	84	85	86	87	88	89	90
91	92	93	94	95	96	97	98	99	100

1. Count by 4s on the chart. Shade each number.

2. Count by 7s on the chart. Circle each number.

3. Which numbers were both shaded and circled?

   ____

4. What patterns do you see in the chart when you count by 4s?

   ____

   ____

5. What patterns do you see when you count by 7s?

   ____

   ____

Mental Math

6. Ellen has 4 robot models. Each model has 5 arms. How many arms are there?

   ______ arms

Notes for Home Your child counted by 4s and by 7s to 100. *Home Activity*: Ask your child to count by 2s and then by 5s on the chart.

Name ______________________

Practice 5-7

Before, After, Between

Use the number line. Answer each question.

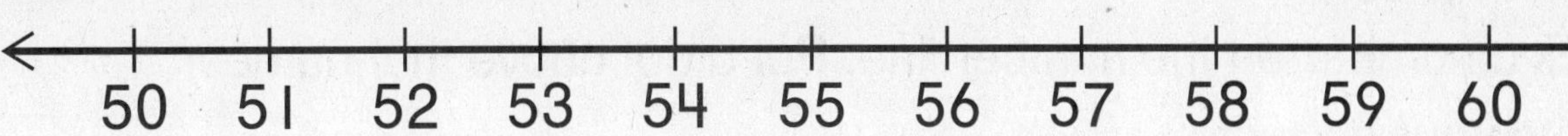

1. Draw a box around the number that is one before 57.

2. Put a line under the number that comes after 52.

3. Circle the number that is between 54 and 56.

4. Put an X on all the numbers that are between 56 and 60.

Answer each question.

5. What number is one before 73? ______

6. What number is one after 27? ______

7. What number is between 93 and 95? ______

8. What number is one before 90? ______

Problem Solving Critical Thinking

9. Solve the riddle.

   I am between 37 and 41.

   I have 4 tens.

   What number am I? ______

   Make up your own riddles for a classmate to solve.

Notes for Home Your child answered questions about numbers. *Home Activity:* Pick a number from the number line on this page. Ask your child to describe it using before, between, and after. (Possible answer: 53 is before 54, 53 is between 52 and 54, and 53 is after 52.)

Name ______________________

Practice 5-8

Find the Nearest Ten

Write your own.

Pick a number on the number line. Put a dot above that number.
Write your answer.

1. 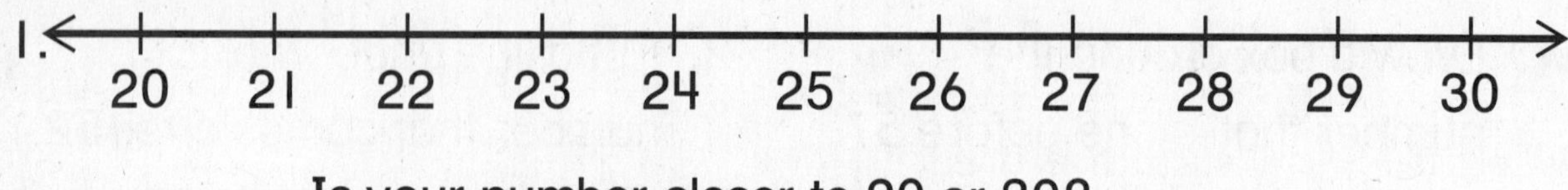

Is your number closer to 20 or 30? _____

2. 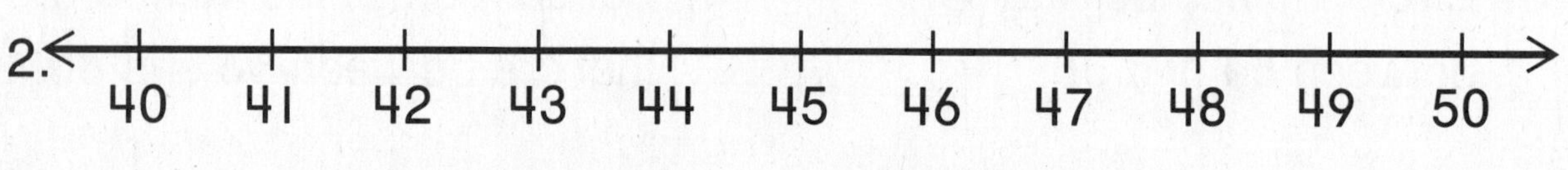

Is your number closer to 40 or 50? _____

3. 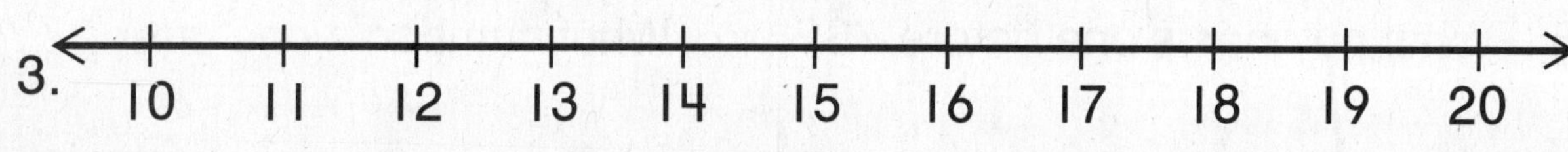

Is your number closer to 10 or 20? _____

For each number, write the nearest ten.

4. 57 60
5. 32 _____
6. 71 _____
7. 24 _____
8. 46 _____
9. 18 _____
10. 93 _____
11. 79 _____

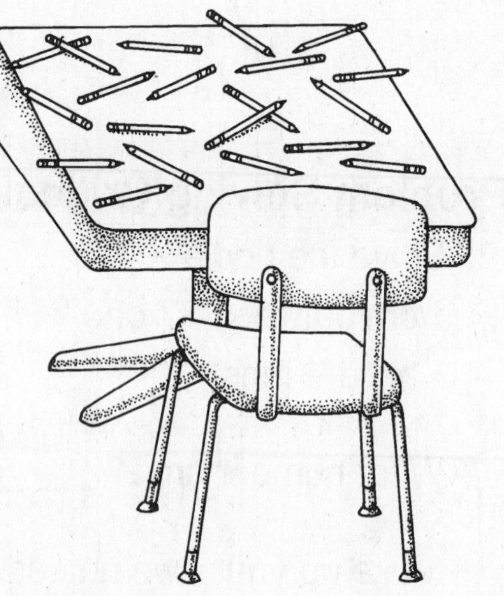

Problem Solving Estimation

12. About how many pencils in all?
Circle you estimate.

About 20 About 50

Notes for Home Your child found the nearest ten. (For example, 40 is the nearest ten for 36.)
Home Activity: Tell your child a number less than 100. Ask him or her to tell you the nearest ten for that number.

 Use with pages 173–174.

Name ____________________

Practice 5-9

Compare Numbers

Circle the number that is least.

1.	38	52	19	2.	27	96	43
3.	61	47	72	4.	81	18	55

Circle the number that is greatest.

5.	76	68	81	6.	91	96	99
7.	45	61	38	8.	51	29	35

Write the numbers in order from least to greatest.

9.	46	18	37	18	37	46
10.	89	56	72	____	____	____
11.	19	65	38	____	____	____
12.	93	48	89	____	____	____

Problem Solving

Three friends sold calendars for their club.
Josh sold 76 calendars.
Jane sold 58 calendars.
June sold the least number of calendars.
How many calendars could June have sold?

____ calendars

Notes for Home Your child compared numbers using *least* and *greatest* and put numbers in order. *Home Activity:* Tell your child 3 numbers less than 100. Ask him or her to put them in order from least to greatest and from greatest to least.

Name ______________________________

Ordinal Numbers

Practice 5-10

1. Color the 1st car blue.
2. Color the 10th car brown.
3. Color the second car red.
4. Color the 7th car orange.
5. Color the 4th car yellow.
6. Color the eighth car purple.

Answer each question.

7. How many cars are behind the 8th car? _____
8. How many cars are behind the 4th car? _____
9. How many cars are in front of the 6th car? _____
10. How many cars are in front of the 10th car? _____

Problem Solving

11. Solve.
    6 children are in front of you.
    7 children are behind you.
    What number are you? _____

Notes for Home Your child used ordinal numbers from 1st through 20th. *Home Activity:* Ask your child to use ordinal numbers to describe the order of something in your home.

Name ______________________

Practice 5-11

Odd and Even Numbers

Write how many in all. Then write **even** or **odd**.

1.

27 ______

2.

______ ______

Write **even** or **odd**.

3. 36 even

4. 47 ______

5. 53 ______

6. 78 ______

Write your own. Write two odd numbers.
Then write two even numbers.

7. Odd numbers: ______ ______

8. Even numbers: ______ ______

Problem Solving Patterns Algebra Readiness

9. Is the number 4,625 odd or even? How do you know?

____

Notes for Home Your child worked with odd and even numbers. *Home Activity:* Ask your child: *I am thinking of an odd number between 56 and 59. What number is it?* (57)

Name ________________________________

Practice 5-12

Problem Solving:
Group Decision Making

1. Work with your group. Collect some items.
   As a group, sort your items the way you like best.
   Decide as a group how to show your sorted items.
   Draw how you sorted them.

Journal

2. Why did you choose this way to sort your items?

Notes for Home Your child made decisions with a group about how to sort items. *Home Activity:* With your child, list 10 items that you see around you. Discuss with your child ways you could sort the items.

Name ______________________________

Practice
Chapter 5
B

Mixed Practice: Lessons 6–12

Count by 3s. Write the numbers.

1. 3, 6, 9, 12, ______, ______, ______, ______

Write the missing numbers.

2. ←|—|—|—|—|—|—|—|—|→

45 46 ____ ____ 49 ____ ____ 52 ____

For each number, write the nearest ten.

3. 47 ______ 4. 82 ______ 5. 64 ______

Write these numbers in order from least to greatest.

6. 76 39 82 ______ ______ ______

Problem Solving

Use the picture to answer the questions.

7. What is the shirt number of the third soccer player? ______

8. What is the shirt number of the fifth soccer player? ______

Journal

9. Are these numbers even or odd? 14 8 26 4
How do you know? ______________________________

Notes for Home Your child practiced number skills from this chapter. *Home Activity:* Ask your child to think of 2 odd numbers less than 100 and tell you how he or she knows they are odd.

Name ______________________

Practice
Chapters 1–5
B

Cumulative Review

Add or subtract.

1.

9	16	15	8	11	9	12
+ 7	− 8	− 7	+ 6	− 4	+ 9	+ 6

Problem Solving

Write the number sentences. Solve.

2. Marsha has 17 books.
Rob has 8 books
How many more books does
Marsha have than Rob?

______________ more books

3. Eric has 13 marbles.
Kate has 7 marbles.
How many more marbles does
Eric have than Kate?

______________ more marbles

Test Prep

Fill in the ○ for the correct answer.

4. Debbie has 11 stickers.
She gives 7 stickers to Joan.
How many stickers does
she have now?

○ 11 − 0 = 11
○ 11 + 7 = 18
○ 11 − 7 = 4
○ 7 + 7 = 14

5. Rachel has 7 hair ribbons.
Janet gives her 8 more.
How many hair ribbons does
Rachel have now?

○ 7 + 7 = 14
○ 8 − 7 = 1
○ 8 + 8 = 16
○ 8 + 7 = 15

Notes for Home Your child reviewed addition and subtraction facts and problem solving. *Home Activity:* Ask you child to tell you a subtraction fact with a difference of 7. (Possible answers: 12 – 5 = 7; 10 – 3 = 7)

Name ___________________________

Practice 6-1

Explore Counting Dimes, Nickels, and Pennies

Count by 10s. Count on by 5s. Count on by ones.

57¢ in all

Use the coins. Count the money. Write the total amount.

1. 

2.     

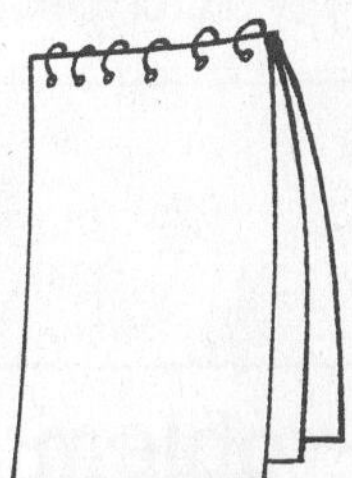

Use these coins. Draw the coins. Write the total amount.

3. 2 dimes, 1 nickel, and 3 pennies

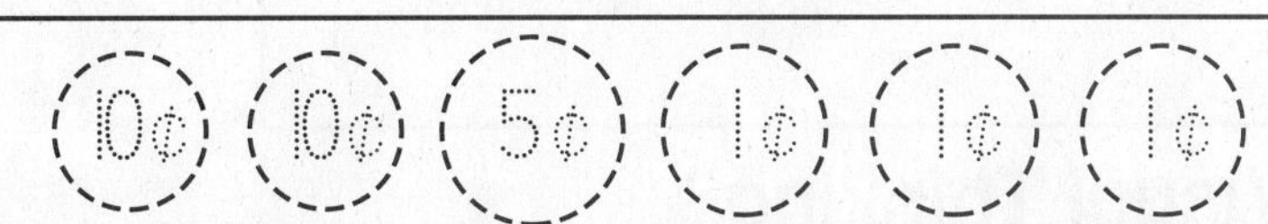

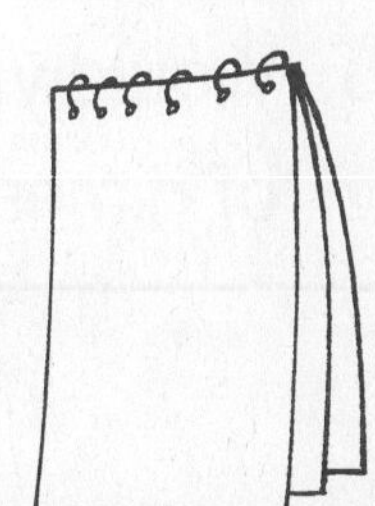

4. 1 dime, 3 nickels, 5 pennies

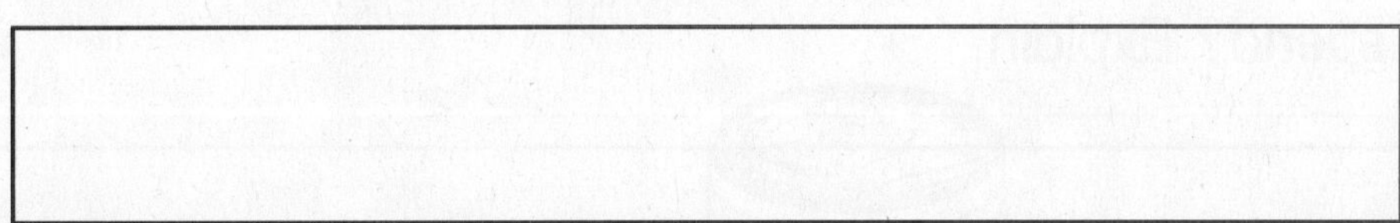

Talk About It Is it easier for you to count coins from greatest value to least, or least to greatest value? Why?

Notes for Home Your child counted groups of dimes, nickels, and pennies. *Home Activity:* Ask your child to draw dimes, nickels, and pennies to show 52¢.

Name ___________________________

Quarters

Practice 6-2

Use coins. Count the money. Write the total amount.

1. 

98¢

2. 

Use these coins. Draw the coins. Write how much in all.

3. 1 quarter, 4 dimes, 1 nickel, and 3 pennies

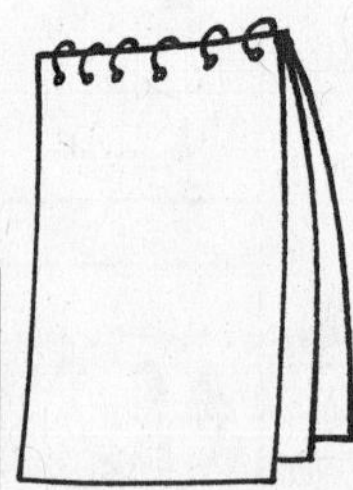

4. You pick 5 coins.

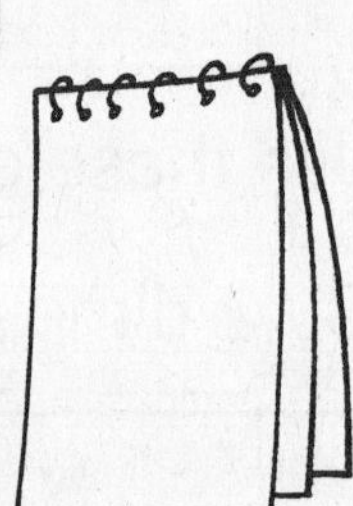

Problem Solving Visual Thinking

5. Would you like to have the stack of nickels or the stack of dimes to spend? Explain.

Notes for Home Your child counted groups of coins that included quarters. *Home Activity:* Tell your child an amount less than a dollar. Have him or her show you this amount using any combinations of quarters, dimes, nickels, and pennies.

Name ___________________________

Practice 6-3

Half Dollars

Fill in the table to show some ways to make 50¢.

Write how many of each coin is used. Use coins to help.

Half dollar	Quarters	Dimes	Nickels	Value of coins
1	0	0	0	50¢
0		0	0	
0		3		50¢
0	1	0		50¢
0	0		0	
0	0	0		
0			8	50¢

Problem Solving

How much could one of these cost?

Choose a price between 50¢ and 79¢.

Draw coins. Write the price.

Notes for Home Your child used coins to show 50¢. *Home Activity:* Ask your child which coins have the greatest value: 10 dimes, 2 quarters, or 1 fifty-cent piece. (They all have the same value.)

Name ________________________________

Practice 6-4

Problem Solving: Make a List

1. Yoko needs 40¢ to buy juice from a vending machine. Use coins. Find all the ways to make 40¢ using quarters, dimes, and nickels.

	Quarter	Dime	Nickel
Use 1 quarter.			
Use 1 quarter again.			

Critical Thinking

Taro has these coins in his hand.
He has 50¢ in all.
What coins could he have in his pocket?

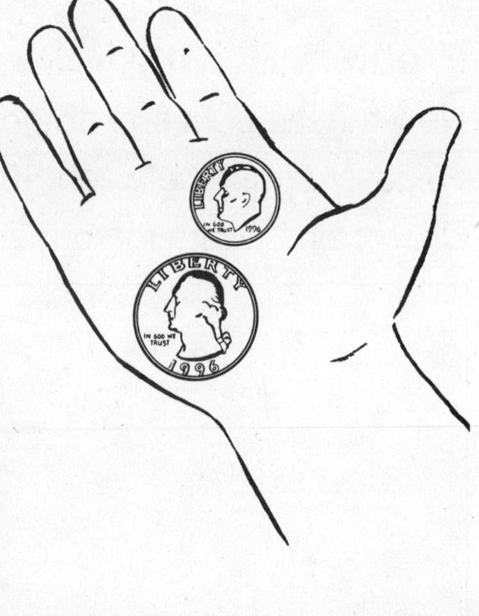

Show 2 ways. Draw the coins.

2.

3.

Notes for Home Your child found ways to make 40¢ and put the information into an organized list. *Home Activity:* Use quarters, dimes, and nickels. Ask your child to show you all the ways to make 50¢. (There are 10 different ways. Possible answers: 2 quarters; 1 quarter and 2 dimes and 1 nickel; 5 dimes; 10 nickels.)

Name ____________________

Mixed Practice: Lessons 1–4

Use coins. Count the money. Write the total amount.

1. 

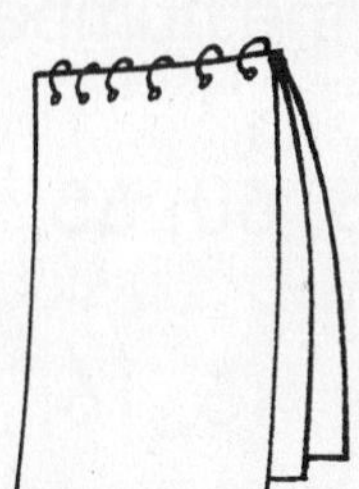

Use these coins. Draw the coins. Write the total amount.

2. 1 half dollar, 1 quarter, 1 dime, 2 nickels, 2 pennies

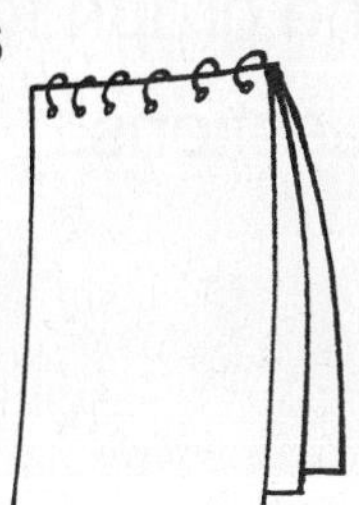

Problem Solving

3. Randi needs 30¢ for a vending machine. Use coins. Find all the ways to make 30¢ using quarters, dimes, and nickels. Make a list.

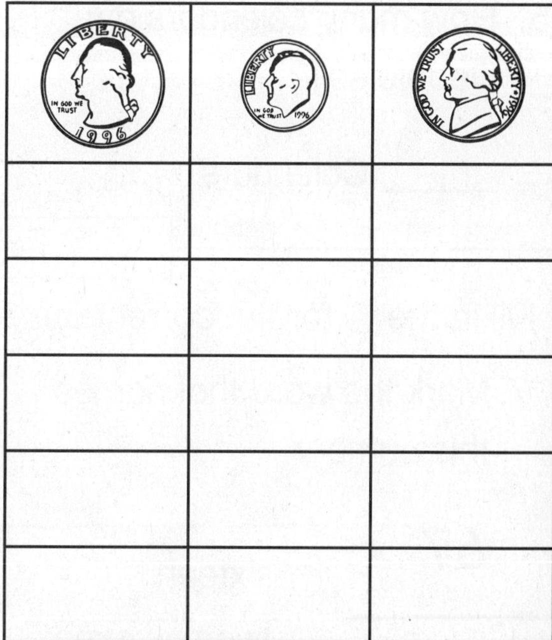

Journal

Choose an amount between 27¢ and 63¢. Write the amount.
Use coins. Show the amount in 2 different ways. Draw the coins.

Notes for Home Your child practiced making a list and counting half dollars, quarters, dimes, nickels, and pennies.
Home Activity: Have your child use coins to show you different ways to make 40¢.

Name ______________________________

Practice
Chapters 1–6
A

Cumulative Review

Count by ones, 5s, or 10s.
Write the numbers.

1. 55, 60, 65, ____, ____, ____

2. 40, 50, 60, ____, ____, ____

3. 14, 15, 16, ____, ____, ____

4. 0, 5, 10, ____, ____, ____

Problem Solving

Use the graph to answer the questions.

School Calendars Sold	
Gloria	XXXXX
Markus	XXXXXXX
Tony	XXX
Debbie	XXXXXX

Each X stands for 5 calendars.

5. How many calendars did Debbie sell?

_____ Calendars

6. How many more calendars did Markus sell than Tony?

_____ more calendars

Test Prep

Fill in the ○ for the correct answer.

7. Mark the word that names this number.

67

○ sixteen
○ twenty-seven
○ sixty-seven
○ sixty

8. Mark the number for this word.

forty

50	14	4	40
○	○	○	○

Notes for Home Your child reviewed skip counting, pictographs, and number words. *Home Activity:* Ask your child to read the graph and tell you who sold the most calendars (Markus) and who sold the next greatest number. (Debbie).

Name ______________________________

Coin Combinations

Practice 6-5

Use the fewest coins to show each amount.

Draw the coins.

1. 

25¢ 

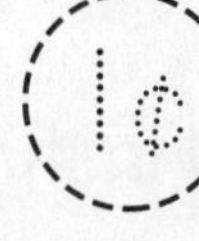

2. 

3. 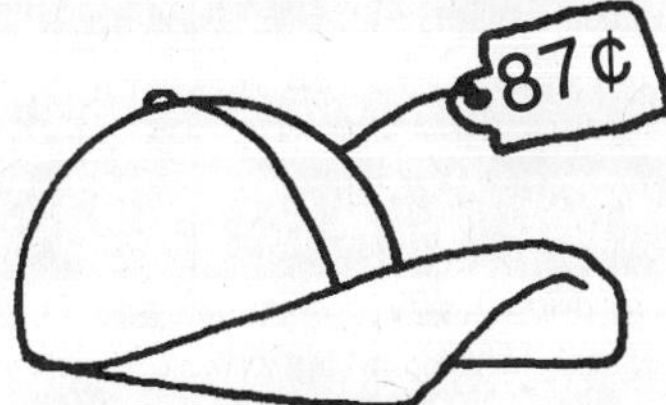

4. 

Problem Solving

5. Draw the same amount of money using the least number of coins.

Notes for Home Your child practiced showing amounts of money using the fewest coins. *Home Activity:* Ask your child to think of an amount between 25¢ and 99¢, and to show the amount using the fewest number of coins.

Name ______________________________

Dollar Bill

Use some , , , and .

Fill in the table to show some ways to make $1.00.
Write how many of each coin is used. Use coins to help.

Half dollar	Quarters	Dimes	Nickels	Value of coins
2	0	0	0	$1.00
0		0	0	$1.00
0	0		0	
0	0	0		$1.00
1		0	0	
1	0		0	
0	3			$1.00
0		3		$1.00
0			5	$1.00

Journal

Pretend that you have $1.00 to spend.
What are some things you could buy that
cost exactly $1.00?

Notes for Home Your child made different coin combinations for $1.00. *Home Activity:* Ask your child how many of each coin it takes to make $1.00: pennies (100), nickels (20), dimes (10), quarters (4), and half-dollars (2).

Name ______________________

Practice 6-7

Problem Solving: Act It Out

Take turns buying and selling. Use dimes to pay for items.
Use pennies to make change.

	Cost	Amount Paid	Change
1.	35¢	4 dimes	5¢
2.			
3.			
4.			
5.			

Problem Solving Critical Thinking

6. Use the picture. Name 2 items you could buy with 8 dimes. How much would you have left over?

____

Notes for Home Your child used coins to make change. *Home Activity:* Ask your child to point to the highest-priced item and the lowest-priced item, and tell how many dimes it would take to buy each. (95¢: 10 dimes; 18¢: 2 dimes)

Name ______________________________

Practice
Chapter 6
B

Mixed Practice: Lessons 5–7

Use the fewest coins to show the amount.

Draw the coins.

1. 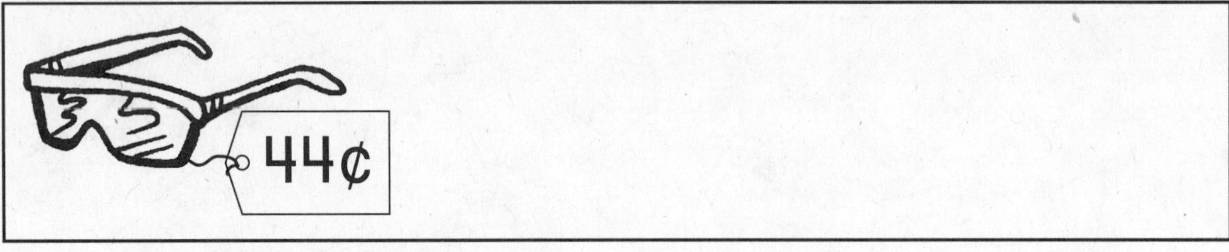

Use some , , , and .

Show 2 ways to make $1.00. Draw the coins.

2. 

3. 

Problem Solving

Solve.

4. Leon has 5 dimes. He buys a model truck for 48¢.How much change should she get back?

______

Journal

5. What coins could you use to pay for something that costs 63¢? What change would you get back?

Notes for Home Your child practiced choosing coins to show amounts of money and making change to solve problems. *Home Activity:* Ask your child to draw 2 other ways to show the amount in Exercise 1.

Name ______________________________

Practice
Chapters 1–6
B

Cumulative Review

For each number, write the nearest ten.

1. Is 56 closer to 50 or 60?

   56 is closer to ______.

2. Is 84 closer to 80 or 90?

   84 is closer to ______.

Write the numbers in order from least to greatest.

3. 83 29 45 ______ ______ ______

Problem Solving

Solve the riddles.

4. I am between 27 and 37.
   I have 5 ones.
   What number am I? ______

5. I am less than 41.
   I have 4 tens.
   What number am I? ______

Test Prep

Fill in the ○ for the correct answer.

6. Which sentence tells about the picture?

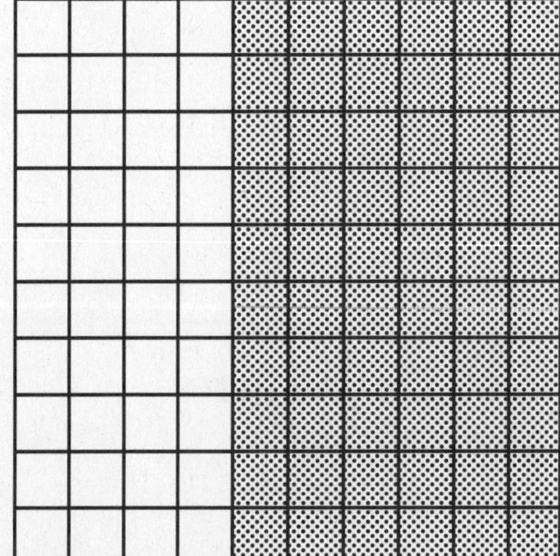

○ 40 and 60 is 100.

○ 35 and 65 is 100.

○ 30 and 70 is 100.

○ 15 and 85 is 100.

Notes for Home Your child reviewed ordering numbers, finding the nearest ten for a number, and solving problems. *Home Activity:* Ask your child to put 48, 27, 51, and 39 in order from least to greatest. (27, 39, 48, 51)

Name ______________________________

Practice 7-1

Explore One Minute

How many times can you do each activity in one minute? Estimate. Then do the activity. Write how many.

1. Write a five-letter word.

   Estimate: ______ times

   How many? ______ times

2. Draw a star.

   Estimate: ______ times

   How many? ______ times

3. Do jumping jacks.

   Estimate: ______ times

   How many? ______ times

4. Bounce a ball.

   Estimate: ______ times

   How many? ______ times

Talk About It Where your estimates accurate? Do you think you could make better estimates now? Why or why not? Compare your answers with a classmate.

Notes for Home Your child estimated how many times he or she could do an activity in one minute. Then he or she timed the activity to check. *Home Activity:* Ask your child to name two other activities that take one minute.

Name ______________________________

Practice 7-2

Estimate Time

Draw an activity you can do in each amount of time.

1. More than one minute

2. Less than one minute

3. About one minute

Tell a Math Story

4. You have one minute to tell someone about school. What would you say?

Notes for Home Your child drew a picture of an activity that would take less than, more than, and about one minute. *Home Activity*: Ask your child to name one more activity for each amount of time.

Name ______________________________

Time to the Hour

Draw the clock hands to show each time.

1. 
5:00

2. 
12:00

3. 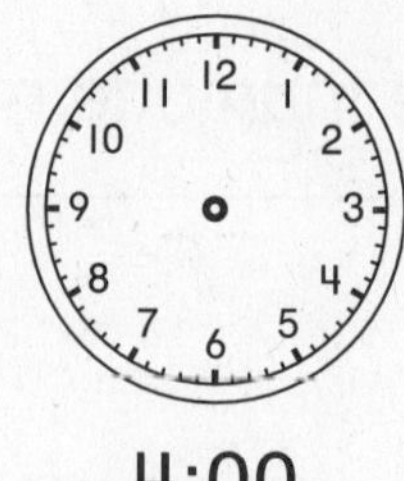
4:00

Write your own. Choose your own time.
Draw the clock hands. Write the time.

4. 
____ :00

5. 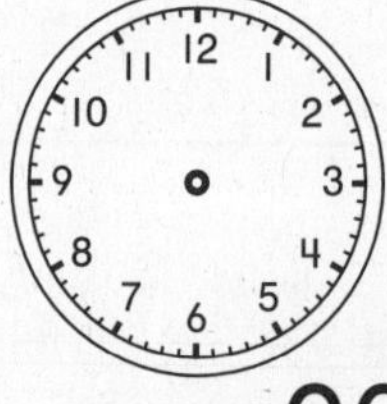
____ :00

6. 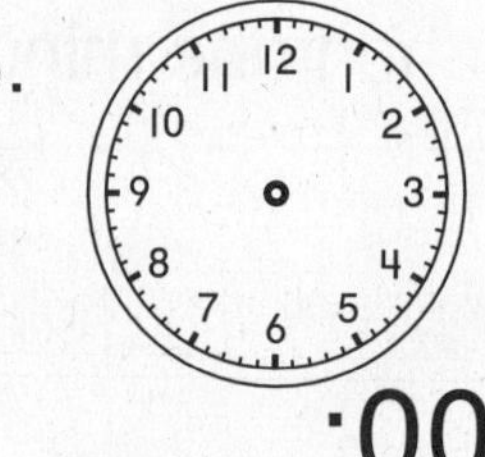
____ :00

Problem Solving Visual Thinking

Look at the picture. What time do you think it is?
Circle the time. How do you know?

7. 
8:00 3:00

8. 
3:00 12:00

Notes for Home Your child showed time to the hour. *Home Activity:* Ask your child to tell where the hour hand and minute hand would be at 4:00. (The minute hand would be at 12, the hour hand at 4.)

Name ______________________

Practice 7-4

Elapsed Time

Use your clock. Draw the clock hands.
Write the ending times.

1. Start 9:00 → 2 hours later → 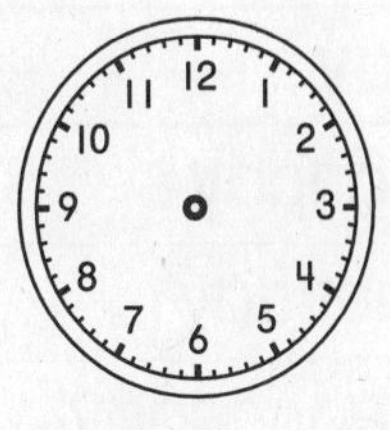 Stop 11:00

2. Start 5:00  → 3 hours later → 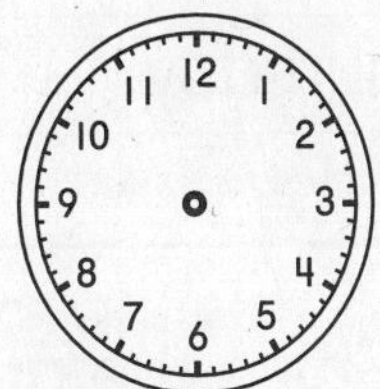 Stop ___:___

Use your clock. When will each activity end?
Write the ending time.

3. Melvin went to a friend's house at 3:00. He left after 1 hour. What time did Melvin leave?

   ___:___.

4. Dena came home from school at 3:00. Her mother came home 2 hours later. They made dinner for 1 hour. What time was it then?

   ___:___.

Problem Solving Critical Thinking

Solve.

5. Tony stopped playing the flute at 7:00. He had played for 1 hour.

   What time did he start playing? ___:___

Notes for Home Your child solved problems involving the passing of time. *Home Activity:* Ask your child to tell you how many hours have gone by between 6:00 and 9:00 in the evening. (3 hours)

Name ______________________________

Practice 7-5

Problem Solving:
Use Data from a Table

School Play Rehearsals		
Day	**Start**	**End**
Monday	2:00	4:00
Tuesday	3:00	5:00
Wednesday	2:00	5:00
Thursday	2:00	6:00
Friday	3:00	6:00

Use the table. Solve the problems.
Write each answer.

1. This Monday, classes end 1 hour before rehearsal begins. What time do classes end?

   1:00

2. On what day is rehearsal the longest? How long is it?

   __________ hours

3. How long is rehearsal on Wednesday?

   ______ hours

4. Which days have rehearsals that last 2 hours?

   ____

   Which days have rehearsals that last 3 hours?

   ____

Journal

5. Copy this table into your journal. Add another column at the right that tells how long rehearsal was each day.

Notes for Home Your child used a table to solve problems. *Home Activity:* Ask your child to tell you how many hours children rehearsed in all. (2 + 2 + 3 + 4 + 3 = 14 hours in all)

Name ___________________________

Mixed Practice: Lessons 1–5

1. Estimate how many times you can count to 20 in one minute. Then do the activity. Write how many.

Estimate: _____ times

How many? _____ times

Write the time.

2. 

___:___

3. 

___:___

Read both clocks.
How many hours have gone by?

4. 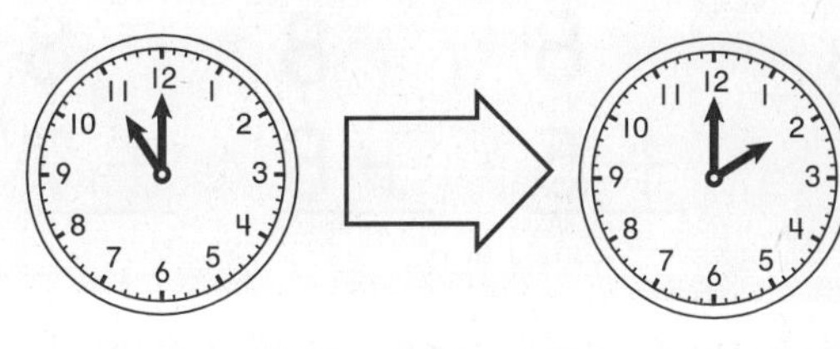

_____ hours

Problem Solving

Use the table.
Answer the question.

Party Times	Start	End
Make crafts	1:00	2:00
Play "Treasure Hunt"	2:00	3:00
Eat a snack	3:00	4:00

5. How long is the party?

_____ hours

Journal

6. Draw two clocks.
Show 8 o'clock on one.
Show 4 hours later on the other.

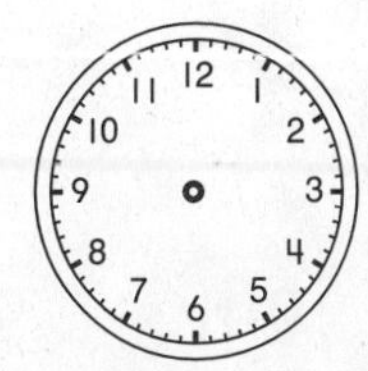

4 hours later

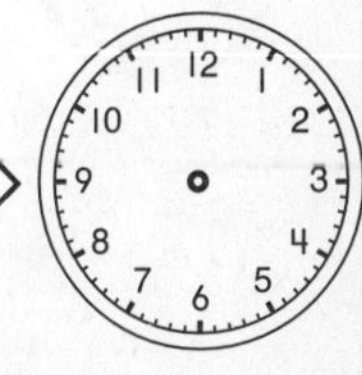

Notes for Home Your child practiced showing and telling time. *Home Activity:* Draw 3 clocks, each with a different time. Ask your child to tell you what time each clock would show 3 hours later.

Name ______________________________

Practice
Chapters 1–7
A

Cumulative Review

Count by 2s. Write the numbers.

1. ____, 14, ____, ____, ____, 22, ____, ____, ____, 30

Count by 5s. Write the numbers.

2. ____, 10, ____, ____, ____, 30, ____, ____

Add or subtract.

3. $\begin{array}{r} 8 \\ +5 \\ \hline \end{array}$ $\begin{array}{r} 8 \\ +8 \\ \hline \end{array}$ $\begin{array}{r} 3 \\ +7 \\ \hline \end{array}$ $\begin{array}{r} 7 \\ +8 \\ \hline \end{array}$ $\begin{array}{r} 5 \\ +4 \\ \hline \end{array}$ $\begin{array}{r} 8 \\ +9 \\ \hline \end{array}$ $\begin{array}{r} 7 \\ +6 \\ \hline \end{array}$

4. $\begin{array}{r} 13 \\ -8 \\ \hline \end{array}$ $\begin{array}{r} 14 \\ -6 \\ \hline \end{array}$ $\begin{array}{r} 15 \\ -7 \\ \hline \end{array}$ $\begin{array}{r} 12 \\ -9 \\ \hline \end{array}$ $\begin{array}{r} 13 \\ -7 \\ \hline \end{array}$ $\begin{array}{r} 17 \\ -8 \\ \hline \end{array}$ $\begin{array}{r} 12 \\ -7 \\ \hline \end{array}$

Test Prep

Fill in the ○ for the correct answer.

Count the money. How much in all?

89¢ ○　94¢ ○　96¢ ○　66¢ ○

Notes for Home Your child reviewed counting by 5s and 10s, addition and subtraction facts, and counting groups of coins. *Home Activity:* Ask your child to count by 10s to 100.

Name ______________________________

Practice 7-6

Tell Time to Five Minutes

Write the time for each clock.

1. 

10:10

2. 

___ : ___

3. 

___ : ___

Draw the minute hand to show the time.

4. 

4:05

5. 

8:50

6. 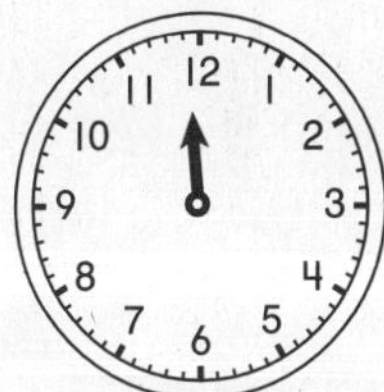

11:55

Problem Solving

Solve. Write the time.

7. The muffins went into the oven at 10 minutes before 4. At what time did they go in the oven?

3: ___

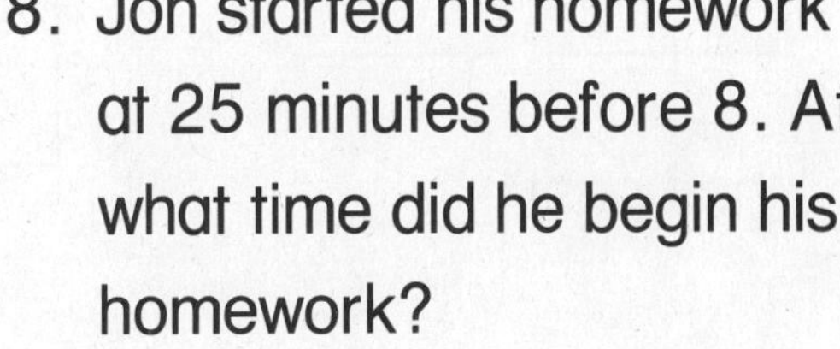

8. Jon started his homework at 25 minutes before 8. At what time did he begin his homework?

___ : ___

Notes for Home Your child told time to 5 minute intervals. *Home Activity:* Ask your child to tell where the minute hand would point at 2:40. (8)

Name ___________________________________

Practice 7-7

Tell Time to the Half Hour

Write the time shown on each clock.

1. 

____

2. 

____

3. 

____

4. 

____

5. 

____

6. 

____

7. **Write your own** time.
Use a half hour.
Draw a picture showing
what you do at that time.

_____ : _____

half past _____

Problem Solving Patterns

8. Write the times to continue the pattern.

7:00, 7:30, 8:00, ___:___, ___:___, ___:___

Notes for Home Your child told time to the half hour. *Home Activity:* Ask your child where the minute hand and the hour hand point at 10:30. (The minute hand points at the 6, the hour hand points between the 10 and 11.)

Name ______________________________

Tell Time to the Quarter Hour

Write the time for each clock.

1. 

12:15

15 minutes after 12

2. 

____ : ____

____ minutes after ____

____ minutes before ____

3. 

____ : ____

half past ____

4. 

____ : ____

____ minutes after ____

____ minutes before ____

Problem Solving Visual Thinking

5. Some watches do not show all the numbers. Write the time shown on this watch.

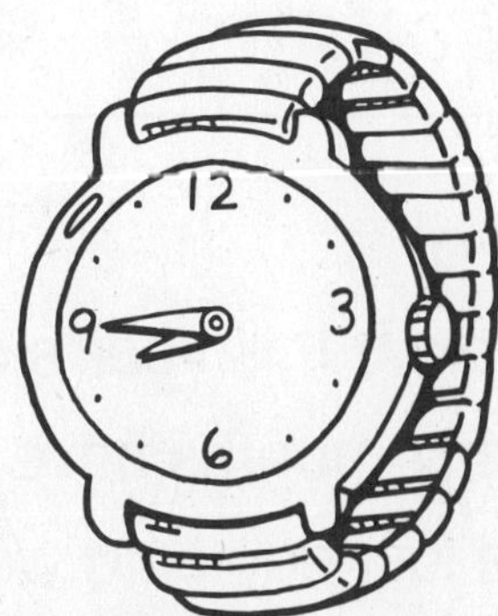

____ : ____

Notes for Home Your child learned how to tell time in 15 minute intervals. *Home Activity:* Ask your child to tell you the time for each 15-minute interval from 7:00 to 8:00. (7:00, 7:15, 7:30, 7:45, 8:00)

Name ________________________________

Practice 7-9

Problem Solving:
Make a Table

1. The calendar shows all the months and days in a year.
   Circle the first and last day of school.
   Circle a month in which a friend or relative has a birthday.

January

S	M	T	W	T	F	S
			1	2	3	4
5	6	7	8	9	10	11
12	13	14	15	16	17	18
19	20	21	22	23	24	25
26	27	28	29	30	31	

February

S	M	T	W	T	F	S
						1
2	3	4	5	6	7	8
9	10	11	12	13	14	15
16	17	18	19	20	21	22
23	24	25	26	27	28	

March

S	M	T	W	T	F	S
						1
2	3	4	5	6	7	8
9	10	11	12	13	14	15
16	17	18	19	20	21	22
23/30	24/31	25	26	27	28	29

April

S	M	T	W	T	F	S
		1	2	3	4	5
6	7	8	9	10	11	12
13	14	15	16	17	18	19
20	21	22	23	24	25	26
27	28	29	30			

May

S	M	T	W	T	F	S
				1	2	3
4	5	6	7	8	9	10
11	12	13	14	15	16	17
18	19	20	21	22	23	24
25	26	27	28	29	30	31

June

S	M	T	W	T	F	S
1	2	3	4	5	6	7
8	9	10	11	12	13	14
15	16	17	18	19	20	21
22	23	24	25	26	27	28
29	30					

July

S	M	T	W	T	F	S
		1	2	3	4	5
6	7	8	9	10	11	12
13	14	15	16	17	18	19
20	21	22	23	24	25	26
27	28	29	30	31		

August

S	M	T	W	T	F	S
					1	2
3	4	5	6	7	8	9
10	11	12	13	14	15	16
17	18	19	20	21	22	23
24/31	25	26	27	28	29	30

September

S	M	T	W	T	F	S
	1	2	3	4	5	6
7	8	9	10	11	12	13
14	15	16	17	18	19	20
21	22	23	24	25	26	27
28	29	30				

October

S	M	T	W	T	F	S
			1	2	3	4
5	6	7	8	9	10	11
12	13	14	15	16	17	18
19	20	21	22	23	24	25
26	27	28	29	30	31	

November

S	M	T	W	T	F	S
						1
2	3	4	5	6	7	8
9	10	11	12	13	14	15
16	17	18	19	20	21	22
23/30	24	25	26	27	28	29

December

S	M	T	W	T	F	S
	1	2	3	4	5	6
7	8	9	10	11	12	13
14	15	16	17	18	19	20
21	22	23	24	25	26	27
28	29	30	31			

2. Make a table using the calendar.
   Use tallies to show how many months have 3 or 4 full weeks.

Months with 3 full weeks	Months with 4 full weeks

Journal

3. Look at this year's calendar. Make a table using tallies to show how many months have the last day on a weekend and how many have the last day on a weekday.

Notes for Home Your child made a table to solve problems. *Home Activity:* Ask your child to show you his or her journal entries and to explain the entries.

Name ______________________________

Practice
Chapter 7
B

Mixed Practice: Lessons 6–9

Write the time for each clock.

1.

___ : ___

___ minutes after ___

2.

___ : ___

half past ___

3.

___ : ___

___ minutes after ___

___ minutes before ___

Write the time for each clock.

4.

___ : ___

5.

___ : ___

Problem Solving

Use the calendar to answer the questions.

March						
S	M	T	W	T	F	S
						1
2	3	4	5	6	7	8
9	10	11	12	13	14	15
16	17	18	19	20	21	22
23/30	24/31	25	26	27	28	29

6. How many Saturdays are in this month? ______

7. On what day of the week is the last day of the month? ___________

Journal

8. Draw two clocks. Show 6:15 on one clock. Show 6:45 on the other clock. Tell how much time has passed. What time will it be in 15 minutes?

Notes for Home Your child told time and used a calendar. *Home Activity*: Ask your child to tell you the time right now. What time will it be in 5 minutes? 15 minutes? 30 minutes? 1 hour?

Name ______________________________

Cumulative Review

Practice Chapters 1–7 B

Use the graph. Answer the questions.

How I Spend My Time on a School Day										
School	▒	▒	▒	▒	▒	▒	▒			
Homework	▒	▒								
Playing	▒	▒	▒ (half)							
Eating	▒	▒	▒ (half)							
Sleeping	▒	▒	▒	▒	▒	▒	▒	▒		
Hours	1	2	3	4	5	6	7	8	9	10

Activity

1. Which activity did this child spend the most time doing?

____

2. What did the child spend about the same time doing?

____

Add or subtract.

3. $\begin{array}{r} 7 \\ +9 \\ \hline \end{array}$ $\begin{array}{r} 17 \\ -8 \\ \hline \end{array}$ $\begin{array}{r} 12 \\ -7 \\ \hline \end{array}$ $\begin{array}{r} 14 \\ -6 \\ \hline \end{array}$ $\begin{array}{r} 7 \\ +5 \\ \hline \end{array}$ $\begin{array}{r} 13 \\ -7 \\ \hline \end{array}$ $\begin{array}{r} 6 \\ +8 \\ \hline \end{array}$

Test Prep

Fill in the ○ for the correct answer.

4. What number completes the table?

Ways to Show 35¢	
Nickels	Dimes
7	0
?	1
3	2
1	3

4 ○ 6 ○ 8 ○ 5 ○

Notes for Home Your child reviewed using a graph, addition and subtraction facts, and making an organized list. *Home Activity:* Ask your child how many hours they spend each day doing the activities in the graph.

Name ______________________

Practice 8-1

Explore Adding Tens

How many in all?

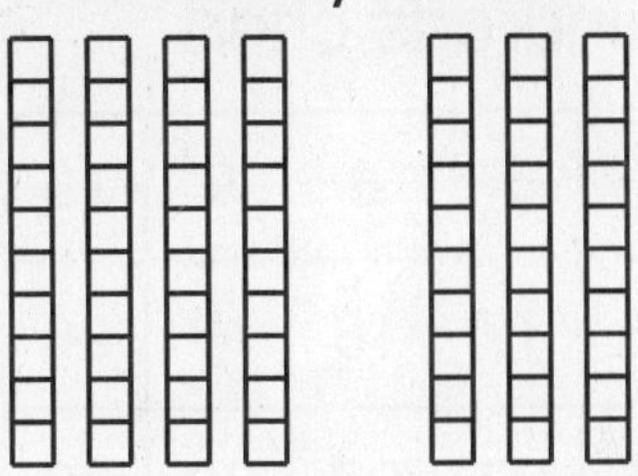

4 tens + 3 tens = 7 tens

40 + 30 = 70

Use [ten-rod] to find how many in all.

1.

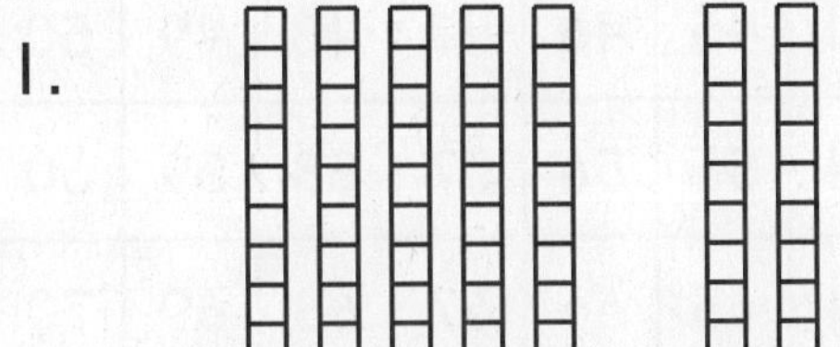

____ tens + ____ tens = ____ tens

____ + ____ = ____

2.

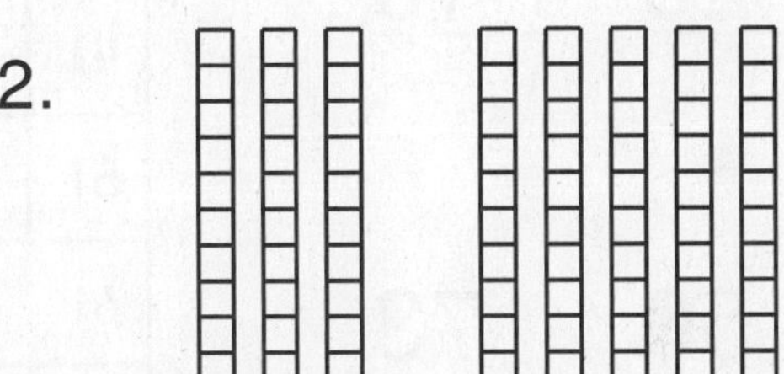

____ tens + ____ tens = ____ tens

____ + ____ = ____

Write your own problems about adding tens.

3. Draw the [ten-rod] you use.

____ tens + ____ tens = ____ tens

____ + ____ = ____

4. Draw the [ten-rod] you use.

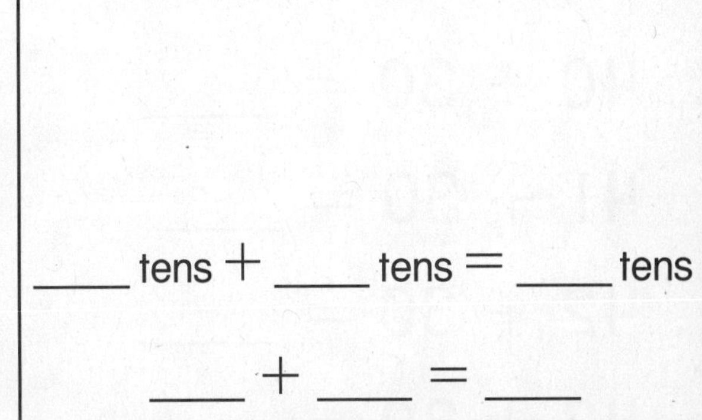

____ tens + ____ tens = ____ tens

____ + ____ = ____

Talk About It Tell a classmate how 4 + 2 and 40 + 20 are alike and how they are different.

Notes for Home Your child explored adding tens. *Home Activity:* Ask your child to tell you the sum of 3 and 3. (6) Then ask him or her to tell you the sum of 30 and 30. (60)

Name ______________________________

Add Tens with a Hundred Chart

Practice 8-2

Add. You can use the hundreds chart.

1. $\begin{array}{r} 34 \\ +\ 10 \\ \hline \end{array}$ $\begin{array}{r} 25 \\ +\ 40 \\ \hline \end{array}$

2. $\begin{array}{r} 68 \\ +\ 20 \\ \hline \end{array}$ $\begin{array}{r} 86 \\ +\ 10 \\ \hline \end{array}$

3. $\begin{array}{r} 50 \\ +\ 30 \\ \hline \end{array}$ $\begin{array}{r} 73 \\ +\ 10 \\ \hline \end{array}$

1	2	3	4	5	6	7	8	9	10
11	12	13	14	15	16	17	18	19	20
21	22	23	24	25	26	27	28	29	30
31	32	33	34	35	36	37	38	39	40
41	42	43	44	45	46	47	48	49	50
51	52	53	54	55	56	57	58	59	60
61	62	63	64	65	66	67	68	69	70
71	72	73	74	75	76	77	78	79	80
81	82	83	84	85	86	87	88	89	90
91	92	93	94	95	96	97	98	99	100

Problem Solving Patterns

4. Add. What patterns do you see?

$40 + 30 =$ ____

$41 + 30 =$ ____

$42 + 30 =$ ____

$43 + 30 =$ ____

$44 + 30 =$ ____

Write your own number sentences to make a pattern.

____ + ____ = ____

____ + ____ = ____

____ + ____ = ____

____ + ____ = ____

____ + ____ = ____

Notes for Home Your child practiced adding tens. *Home Activity:* Ask your child to show you a pattern that starts with the number sentence 20 + 20 = ___. (Possible answers : 21 + 20 = 41, 22 + 20 = 42, 23 + 20 = 43, and so on.)

Name ________________________________

Practice 8-3

Add Using Mental Math

Use mental math to add.

1. 14 + 30 = 44   56 + 20 = ____
2. 37 + 40 = ____   29 + 50 = ____
3. 63 + 20 = ____   82 + 10 = ____
4. 55 + 30 = ____   72 + 20 = ____
5. 75 + 10 = ____   41 + 30 = ____

Problem Solving Patterns

Add. Use mental math. Then write the number sentences to continue the patterns.

6. 22 + 20 = ____
   22 + 30 = ____
   22 + 40 = ____
   ____ + ____ = ____
   ____ + ____ = ____

7. 48 + 10 = ____
   48 + 20 = ____
   48 + 30 = ____
   ____ + ____ = ____
   ____ + ____ = ____

8. Describe the patterns you see.

____

____

Notes for Home Your child practiced using mental math to add. *Home Activity:* Ask your child to tell you how old he or she will be 10 years from now, 20 years from now, and 30 years from now.

Name ______________________________

Practice 8-4

Estimate Two-Digit Sums

Find the nearest ten. Estimate the sum.

1\. Think:

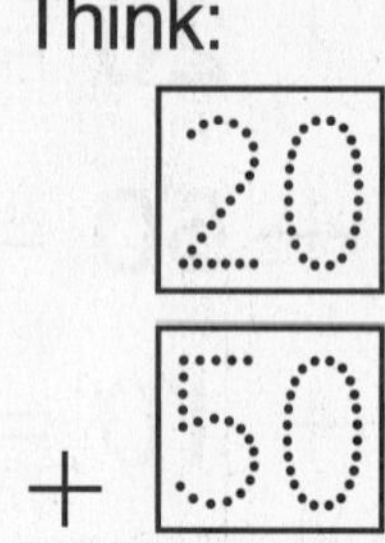

$$\begin{array}{r} 21 \\ +\ 48 \\ \hline \end{array} \qquad \begin{array}{r} 20 \\ +\ 50 \\ \hline 70 \end{array}$$

21 + 48 is about 70.

2\. Think:

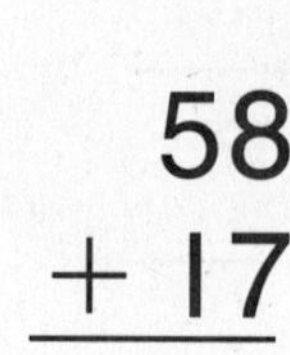

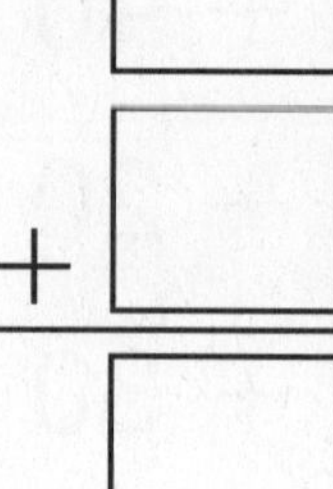

$$\begin{array}{r} 58 \\ +\ 17 \\ \hline \end{array} \qquad \begin{array}{r} \square \\ +\ \square \\ \hline \square \end{array}$$

58 + 17 is about _____.

3\. Think:

$$\begin{array}{r} 33 \\ +\ 22 \\ \hline \end{array} \qquad \begin{array}{r} \square \\ +\ \square \\ \hline \square \end{array}$$

33 + 22 is about _____.

4\. Think:

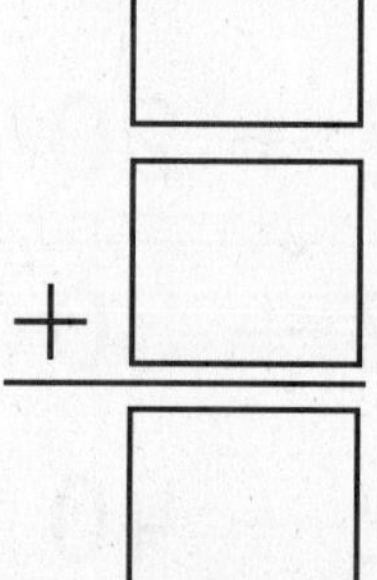

$$\begin{array}{r} 48 \\ +\ 41 \\ \hline \end{array} \qquad \begin{array}{r} \square \\ +\ \square \\ \hline \square \end{array}$$

48 + 41 is about _____.

Problem Solving Estimation

5\. This graph shows how many children chose sandwiches for lunch yesterday. About how many children chose sandwiches for lunch? _____
About how many chose turkey sandwiches? _____

Sandwiches Eaten

Number of Children: 0, 10, 20, 30, 40

Turkey | Tuna Fish

Notes for Home Your child used nearest tens to estimated sums. *Home Activity:* Ask your child to tell you how to estimate the sum of 32 and 18. (32 is about 30 and 18 is about 20. 30 plus 20 is 50.)

Name ______________________________

Practice 8-5

Problem Solving: Make Predictions

1. Predict. Which fruit do you think your classmates like best?

____

2. Why do you think so?

____

____

3. Ask your classmates. Record the results.

Fruit	Tally	Total

4. Was your prediction close? ______________

Critical Thinking

5. What do you think you can do to make better predictions?

Notes for Home Your child made a prediction and then found information to test the prediction. *Home Activity:* Have your child make a prediction and then test it. Predict how many people or how many birds will you see in the next 15 minutes.

Name ______________________

Practice 8-6

Explore Addition With or Without Regrouping

15 children ride bikes to school. 8 children walk.
How many children in all?

Tens	Ones

Start with 15.

Tens	Ones

Add 8.

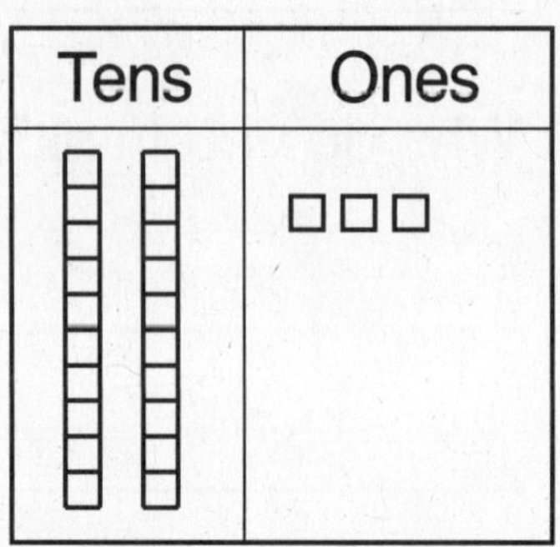

Regroup 10 ones as 1 ten.

Write how many in all. __2__ tens __3__ ones __23__ in all

Use tens/ones mat, tens rods, and ones cubes.

1. Show 26. Add 9.
   How many in all?

   ______ tens ______ ones

   ______ in all

2. Show 48. Add 5.
   How many in all?

   ______ tens ______ ones

   ______ in all

3. Show 12. Add 5.
   How many in all?

   ______ ten ______ ones

   ______ in all

4. Show 37. Add 8.
   How many in all?

   ______ tens ______ ones

   ______ in all

Talk About It Explain to a classmate when it is important to regroup.

Notes for Home Your child explored regrouping in addition. *Home Activity:* Have your child use dry beans or macaroni to show how to regroup when adding 16 and 7. (6 + 7 = 1 ten and 3 ones; 16 + 7 = 23)

Name ______________________

Practice 8-7

Add With or Without Regrouping

Use [tens | ones], [ten rod], and [unit cube].

	Show this many.	Add this many.	Do you need to regroup?	Solve.
1.	27	5	yes	27 + 5 = ____
2.	45	3		45 + 3 = ____
3.	58	8		58 + 8 = ____
4.	34	7		34 + 7 = ____
5.	75	4		75 + 4 = ____
6.	13	9		13 + 9 = ____
7.	66	6		66 + 6 = ____

Problem Solving Critical Thinking

8. Which one-digit numbers can you add to 15 without needing to regroup? How do you know?

____

____

Notes for Home Your child decided when to regroup to add numbers and then found the sums. *Home Activity:* Ask your child to show you two addition problems, one where you must regroup and one where you do not have to regroup. (Possible answer: you must regroup for 15 + 6; you do not regroup for 15 + 4.)

Name ________________________________

Record Addition

Practice 8-8

Add. Then circle the exercise if you regrouped.

Use tens/ones mat, ten rods, and unit cubes

1.
tens	ones
☐	
4	3
+	7
5	0

2.
tens	ones
☐	
3	7
+	1

3.
tens	ones	tens	ones	tens	ones	tens	ones
☐		☐		☐		☐	
5	3	7	2	6	1	4	5
+	8	+	4	+	9	+	7

4.
tens	ones	tens	ones	tens	ones	tens	ones
☐		☐		☐		☐	
3	9	8	6	2	5	1	8
+	6	+	3	+	8	+	4

Problem Solving Critical Thinking

5. Lenny dropped grape jam on his math paper. Now Lenny cannot read some of the numbers. What could the missing numbers be? How do you know?

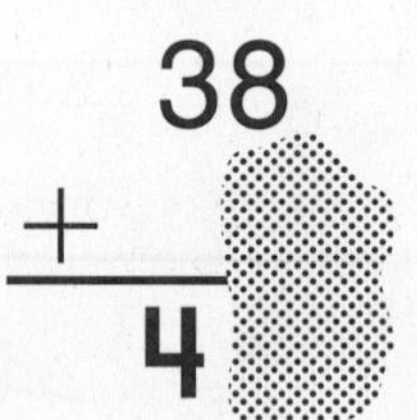

38
+
4

Notes for Home Your child added tens and ones where regrouping was sometime required. *Home Activity:* Ask your child to write addition problems where regrouping is and is not required, and explain his or her reasoning.

 Use with pages 285–286.

Name ______________________________

Practice Chapter 8 A

Mixed Practice: Lessons 1–8

Estimate the sum.

1. Think:

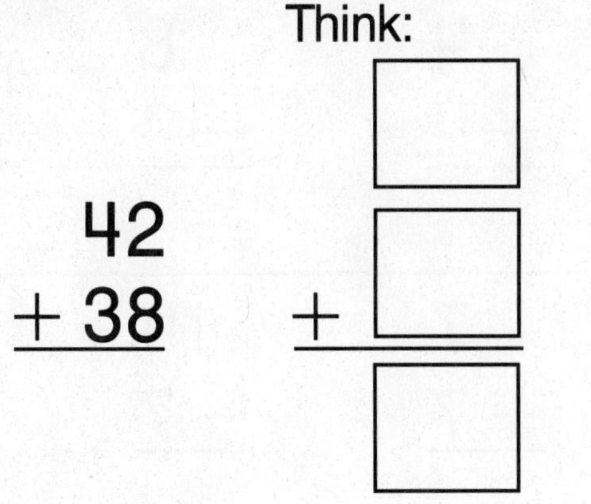

42 + 38 is about _____.

Add. Use mental math.

2. 38 + 20 = _____

42 + 50 = _____

19 + 30 = _____

Problem Solving

3. Complete the chart. Fill in the totals.

Color of Shirts	Tally	Totals
yellow	~~////~~ /	
red	~~////~~ ////	
white	///	

4. Ms. April's class made a chart to show the color of shirts worn by the students. What color shirt would you predict to see most often in Mr. May's class? ____________________

Journal

6. Make a chart to show the color of shirts worn by the students in your class. What color shirt do you see most often?

Notes for Home Your child practiced adding tens, using mental math, estimating sums, and solving problems. *Home Activity:* Have your child look at Exercise 2 and tell you which of the problems has the greater sum and why.

Name ______________________________

Practice
Chapters 1–8
A

Cumulative Review

Add or subtract.

1. $5 + 5 =$ ____ $10 - 5 =$ ____

2. $4 + 4 =$ ____ $8 - 4 =$ ____

3. $6 + 6 =$ ____ $12 - 6 =$ ____

4. $7 + 7 =$ ____ $14 - 7 =$ ____

Write how many. Then write **even** or **odd**.

5. ____ ________

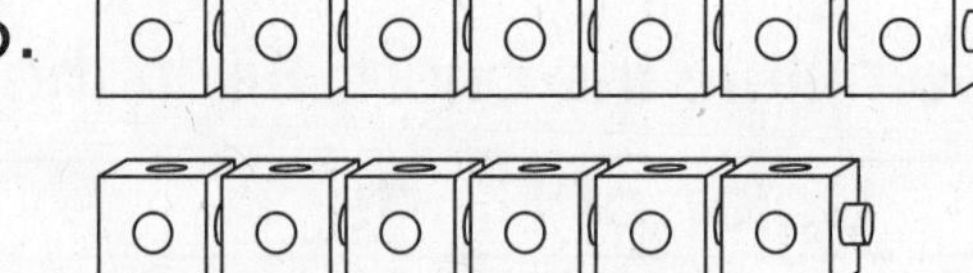

6. ____ ________

Test Prep

Fill in the ○ for the correct answer.

Use the picture to answer the questions.

7. Which is clown C?
   - ○ first
   - ○ second
   - ○ third
   - ○ fourth

8. Which is clown E?
   - ○ second
   - ○ third
   - ○ fifth
   - ○ sixth

Notes for Home Your child reviewed concepts from earlier chapters. *Home Activity:* Ask your child which clown in the picture is first and which is last. (Clown A is first and clown F is last.)

Name ____________________

Practice 8-9

Add Two-Digit Numbers With or Without Regrouping

Use tens/ones mat, tens, and ones. Regroup if you need to.

1.

tens	ones	tens	ones	tens	ones	tens	ones
1		☐		☐		☐	
2	5	4	6	7	1	3	5
+ 1	7	+ 2	3	+ 1	5	+ 4	7
4	2						

2.

tens	ones	tens	ones	tens	ones	tens	ones
☐		☐		☐		☐	
5	9	8	6	1	7	6	4
+ 3	6	+ 1	2	+ 4	8	+ 2	6

3.

tens	ones	tens	ones	tens	ones	tens	ones
☐		☐		☐		☐	
3	9	5	8	7	4	4	1
+ 2	6	+ 4	1	+ 1	9	+ 3	9

Problem Solving Visual Thinking

4. We started with this. | Now we have this. | Draw what was added.

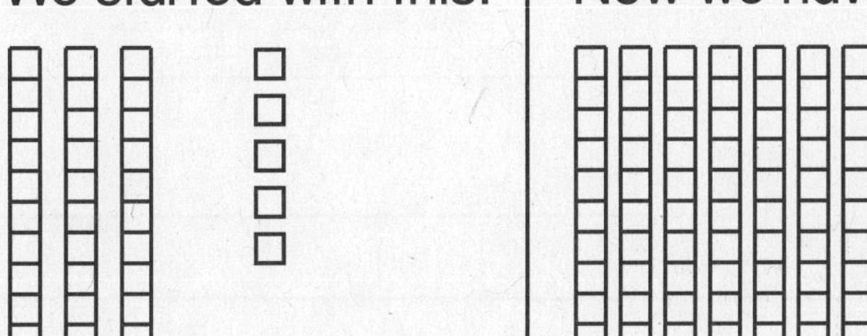

Notes for Home Your child added two-digit numbers with and without regrouping. *Home Activity:* Have your child use dried beans or macaroni to explain why it sometimes is necessary to regroup.

Name ______________________

Practice 8-10

Add Two-Digit Numbers

Add. Regroup if you need to.

1. $\begin{array}{r} 27 \\ +\ 24 \\ \hline \end{array}$ $\begin{array}{r} 52 \\ +\ \ 9 \\ \hline \end{array}$ $\begin{array}{r} 34 \\ +\ 57 \\ \hline \end{array}$ $\begin{array}{r} 19 \\ +\ 43 \\ \hline \end{array}$ $\begin{array}{r} 44 \\ +\ 55 \\ \hline \end{array}$

2. $\begin{array}{r} 51 \\ +\ 29 \\ \hline \end{array}$ $\begin{array}{r} 73 \\ +\ 16 \\ \hline \end{array}$ $\begin{array}{r} 18 \\ +\ 36 \\ \hline \end{array}$ $\begin{array}{r} 35 \\ +\ 55 \\ \hline \end{array}$ $\begin{array}{r} 67 \\ +\ 11 \\ \hline \end{array}$ $\begin{array}{r} 33 \\ +\ 38 \\ \hline \end{array}$

3. $\begin{array}{r} 14 \\ +\ 66 \\ \hline \end{array}$ $\begin{array}{r} 68 \\ +\ 27 \\ \hline \end{array}$ $\begin{array}{r} 26 \\ +\ 72 \\ \hline \end{array}$ $\begin{array}{r} 57 \\ +\ 15 \\ \hline \end{array}$ $\begin{array}{r} 35 \\ +\ 36 \\ \hline \end{array}$ $\begin{array}{r} 40 \\ +\ 49 \\ \hline \end{array}$

Problem Solving

4. Kevin's apples weigh 32 pounds. Which two baskets are his?

____

Write your own math story about the apple baskets. Ask a friend to solve it.

____

____

____

____

Notes for Home Your child added two-digit numbers with and without regrouping. *Home Activity:* Have your child tell you how to find the sum of 46 + 25. (Add the ones. 6 + 5 = 11. Regroup. Add the tens. 1 + 4 + 2 = 7. The sum is 71.)

 Use with pages 291–292.

Name ______________________________

Practice 8-11

Add Money

Add.

1. 14¢	43¢	27¢	48¢	35¢	57¢
+ 18¢	+ 25¢	+ 53¢	+ 24¢	+ 44¢	+ 24¢
32¢					

2. 61¢	83¢	78¢	35¢	57¢	82¢
+ 29¢	+ 16¢	+ 16¢	+ 63¢	+ 31¢	+ 10¢

Mixed Practice Add.

3. 45¢	21¢	37	13	56¢	78
+ 38¢	+ 49¢	+ 26	+ 57	+ 19¢	+ 7

4. 62	34¢	18	25¢	70	18¢
+ 24	+ 7¢	+ 63	+ 39¢	+ 16	+ 13¢

Problem Solving Critical Thinking

5. Peg has 75¢. Which two items could she buy?

__________ and __________

Notes for Home Your child added amounts of money up to 99¢. *Home Activity:* Ask your child: *How much money would you have in all if you had 25¢ and 38¢?* (63¢)

Name ________________________________

Practice 8-12

Add Three Numbers

Add.

1.	37	64	43	16	24	10
	23	14	32	51	25	20
	+ 12	+ 19	+ 8	+ 13	+ 35	+ 30
	72					

2.	21	54	18	45	37	56
	17	12	31	23	42	31
	+ 31	+ 26	+ 8	+ 11	+ 1	+ 4

3.	14	68	26	52	35	16
	31	10	32	11	34	17
	+ 6	+ 7	+ 24	+ 15	+ 6	+ 10

Problem Solving Critical Thinking

The shelf cannot hold more than 90 pounds. How many pounds can be in the last box?

________ pounds

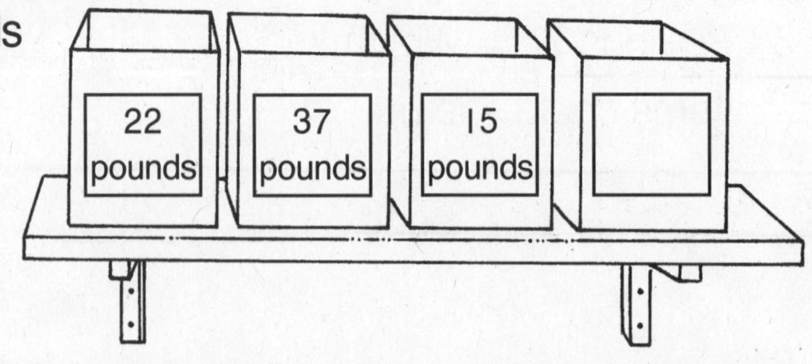

Notes for Home Your child has found the sum of 3 numbers. *Home Activity:* Ask your child to explain his or her reasoning for solving the Problem Solving exercise.

Name ______________________________

Problem Solving: Guess and Check

Practice 8-13

Solve. Show and check each guess.

1. Libis has 58¢.
   She wants to buy two toys.
   What can she buy?

   Libis can buy the ______________ and the ______________.

2. Which other two toys can
   Libis buy with 58¢?

   Libis can buy the ______________ and the ______________.

3. Armando has 50¢.
   He wants to buy two toys.
   What can he buy?

   Armando can buy the ______________ and the ______________.

Estimation

4. Libis wants to buy 3 toys. Does she have enough money?
   How do you know?

   ____

   ____

Notes for Home Your child solved problems by guessing and testing. *Home Activity:* Ask your child if it is possible to buy 3 toys with 70¢. (Yes, you can buy toys B, D, and F for less than 70¢.)

Name ______________________________

Practice
Chapter 8
B

Mixed Practice: Lessons 9–13

Add. Regroup if you need to.

1.						
	26	58	32	16	45	27
	+ 12	+ 29	+ 48	+ 33	+ 29	+ 18

2.					
	34¢	51¢	15¢	63¢	22¢
	+ 49¢	+ 16¢	+ 28¢	+ 17¢	+ 51¢

3.						
	42	37	25	51	11	30
	15	43	23	24	50	46
	+ 15	+ 7	+ 22	+ 19	+ 6	+ 13

Problem Solving

Solve. Show and check each guess.

4. Sue has 56¢.
   She wants to buy two toys.
   What can she buy?

   She can buy the ________ and the ________.

Journal

5. How does making a guess that is not the answer help you make the next guess?

Notes for Home Your child reviewed adding two-digit numbers with and without regrouping, adding three numbers, and using the strategy of guess and check to solve problems. *Home Activity:* Ask your child how much money he or she would need to buy the two most expensive toys shown in Exercise 4. (31¢ + 38¢ = 69¢.)

Name ____________________

Practice
Chapters 1–8
B

Cumulative Review

Circle the numbers you would add first.

Look for doubles and numbers that make 10. Add.

1.

4	8	5	1	4	3
5	1	3	7	5	6
+ 6	+ 2	+ 5	+ 9	+ 4	+ 7

Draw coins. Show two different ways to make 75¢.

2.

3.

Draw coins. Show two different ways to make 30¢.

4.

5.

Test Prep

Fill in the ○ for the correct answer.

Which group of numbers is in order from the least to the greatest?

6. ○ 27, 36, 58, 45
   ○ 24, 22, 18, 9
   ○ 48, 66, 75, 80
   ○ 53, 70, 68, 92

7. ○ 18, 28, 31, 16
   ○ 12, 22, 32, 23
   ○ 25, 37, 26, 38
   ○ 39, 40, 78, 87

Notes for Home Your child reviewed skills from earlier chapters. *Home Activity:* Ask your child to think of 3 numbers that have a sum less than 10. (Possible answers: 1 + 2 + 3, 2 + 5 + 2, 4 + 4 + 1, and so on.)

Name ____________________

Explore Subtracting Tens

Use [tens block] to find how many are left.

1. 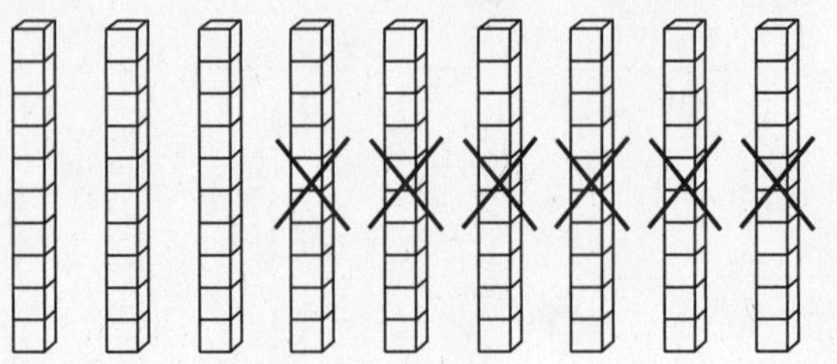

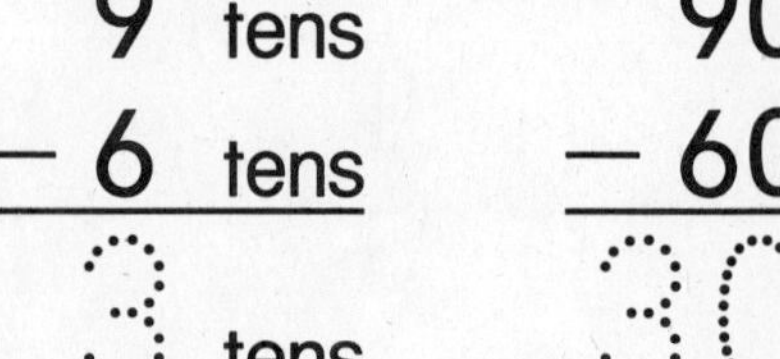

9 tens		90
− 6 tens		− 60
3 tens		30

2. 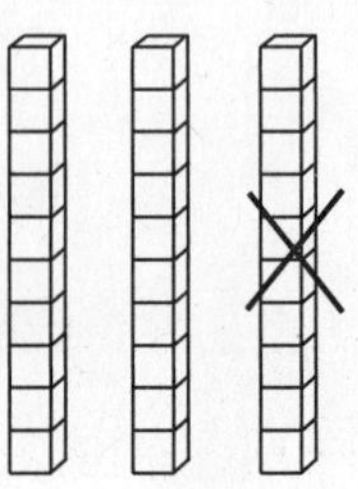

3 tens		30
− 1 tens		− 10
____ tens		____

3. 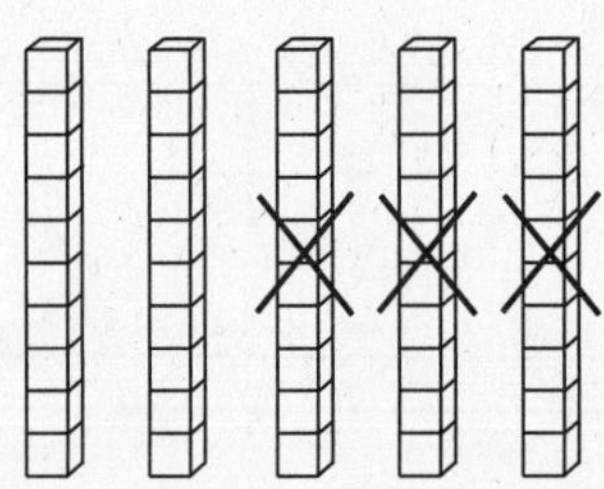

5 tens		50
− 3 tens		− 30
____ tens		____

Subtract. You can use [tens block] to help.

4.

7 tens		70
− 2 tens		− 20
____ tens		____

5.

6 tens		60
− 4 tens		− 40
____ tens		____

Talk About It How does finding 9 − 6 help you find 90 − 60?

Notes for Home Your child explored subtracting tens. *Home Activity:* Ask your child to find 5 tens minus 2 tens and then 50 minus 20. (3 tens, 30)

Name ______________________

Practice 9-2

Subtract Tens With a Hundred Chart

Subtract. You can use the hundred chart.

1. 56 − 20 = 36

2. 94 − 50 = ____

3. 35 − 10 = ____

4. 73 − 40 = ____

1	2	3	4	5	6	7	8	9	10
11	12	13	14	15	16	17	18	19	20
21	22	23	24	25	26	27	28	29	30
31	32	33	34	35	36	37	38	39	40
41	42	43	44	45	46	47	48	49	50
51	52	53	54	55	56	57	58	59	60
61	62	63	64	65	66	67	68	69	70
71	72	73	74	75	76	77	78	79	80
81	82	83	84	85	86	87	88	89	90
91	92	93	94	95	96	97	98	99	100

5.

64	27	88	49	61	78	54
− 30	− 10	− 30	− 20	− 40	− 50	− 20

Problem Solving Patterns

6. Subtract.

70 − 20 = ____

70 − 30 = ____

70 − 40 = ____

Write your own number sentences to make a pattern.

____ − ____ = ____

____ − ____ = ____

____ − ____ = ____

Notes for Home Your child subtracted tens on a hundred chart. *Home Activity:* Ask your child to show you how he or she used the hundred chart to subtract tens.

Name ______________________________

Practice 9-3

Estimate Two-Digit Differences

Find the nearest ten. Estimate the difference.

1.

```
  67
- 43
```

Think: 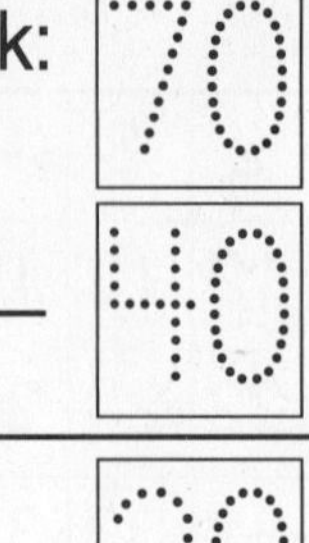

70 − 40 = 30

67 − 43 is about 30.

2.

```
  84
- 36
```

Think: ☐ − ☐ = ☐

84 − 36 is about _____.

3.

```
  43
- 27
```

Think: 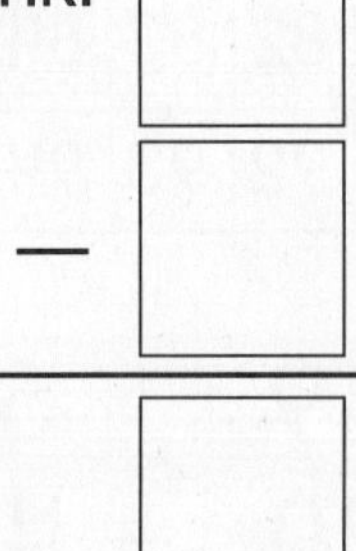

☐ − ☐ = ☐

43 − 27 is about _____.

4.

```
  58
- 27
```

Think: ☐ − ☐ = ☐

58 − 27 is about _____.

Problem Solving Estimation

Find the nearest ten. Estimate the difference.

5. The giant squid is about 17 meters long.
The whale shark is about 13 meters long.
About how much longer is the squid than the shark?

About _____ meters

Notes for Home Your child used nearest tens to estimate differences. *Home Activity:* Ask your child to tell you how to estimate 81–22. (81 is about 80 and 22 is about 20. 80 minus 20 is 60.)

Name ______________________________

Explore Subtraction With or Without Regrouping

Samantha counted 40 pennies in her piggy bank.
She gave 9 pennies to her younger brother.
How many pennies does she have now?

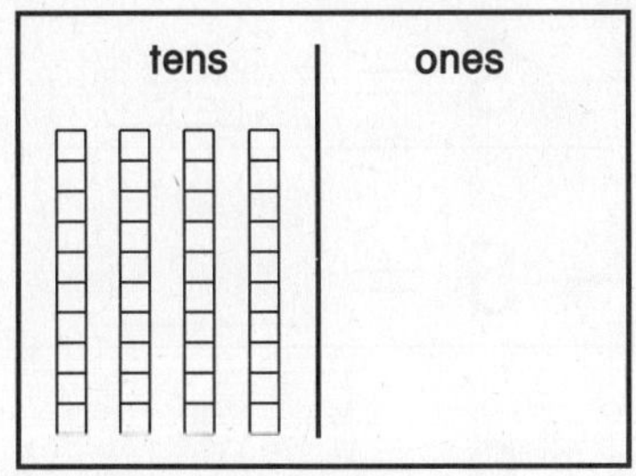

Start with 40.

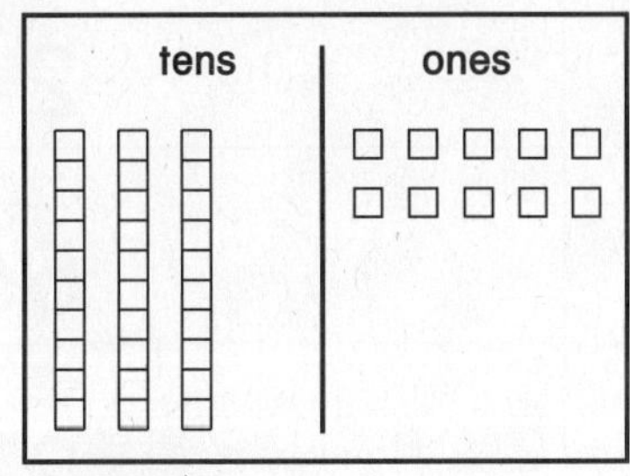

Regroup 1 ten as 10 ones.

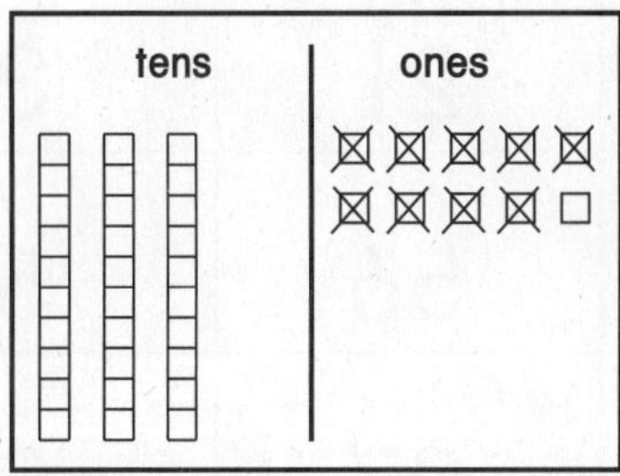

Subtract 9.

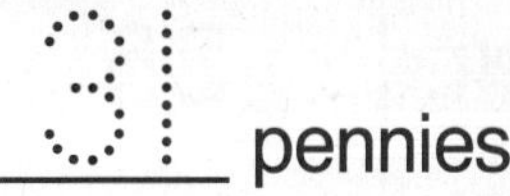

___ pennies

Use [tens ones mat], [ten rod], and [ones cube].

Find how many are left.

1. Show 56. Subtract 8.

   4 tens 8 ones

   48

2. Show 37. Subtract 9.

   ____ tens ____ ones

   ____

3. Show 73. Subtract 6.

   ____ tens ____ ones

   ____

4. Show 26. Subtract 7.

   ____ tens ____ ones

   ____

Talk About It How does regrouping help you subtract?

Notes for Home Your child explored regrouping with subtraction. *Home Activity:* Have your child show how he or she regrouped to find the difference for Exercise 2.

Name ________________________________

Practice 9-5

Subtract With or Without Regrouping

Use [tens | ones mat], [tens rod], and [ones cube].

	Show this many.	Subtract this many.	Do you need to regroup?	Solve.
1.	21	3	yes	21 − 3 = 18
2.	56	5		56 − 5 = ____
3.	27	9		27 − 9 = ____
4.	35	7		35 − 7 = ____
5.	44	3		44 − 3 = ____
6.	18	7		18 − 7 = ____
7.	42	4		42 − 4 = ____
8.	33	2		33 − 2 = ____
9.	11	8		11 − 8 = ____

Problem Solving Critical Thinking

10. Which numbers in the first column above can you subtract from 75 without needing to regroup? For which numbers would you need to regroup? How do you know? ________________________________

____

Notes for Home Your child decided when to regroup to subtract. *Home Activity:* Ask your child to show you two subtraction problems, one with regrouping and one without regrouping.

Name ___________________________

Record Subtraction

Practice 9-6

Subtract. You can use [tens | ones mat], [tens rod], and [ones cube] to help.

Then circle the difference if you regrouped.

1.

tens	ones
□	□
5	3
−	7
4	6

tens	ones
□	□
6	7
−	6

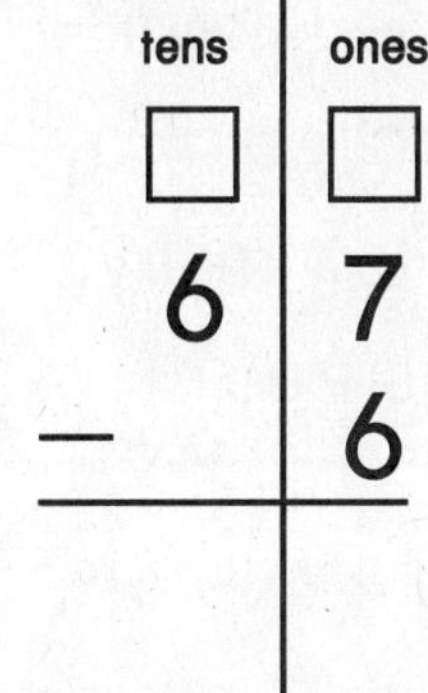

2.

tens	ones
□	□
3	2
−	4

tens	ones
□	□
7	4
−	3

tens	ones
□	□
6	7
−	8

tens	ones
□	□
5	3
−	5

Problem Solving Patterns

Subtract. What patterns do you see?

3. $67 - 8 =$ ___ $67 - 18 =$ ___ $67 - 28 =$ ___ $67 - 38 =$ ___ $67 - 48 =$ ___

Notes for Home Your child regrouped and wrote the differences for subtraction problems. *Home Activity:* Ask your child to explain his or her answer for one of the exercises on this page.

Name ______________________________

Practice 9-7

Problem Solving:
Choose a Computation Method

Choose a strategy. Draw the blocks or write the number sentences.

1. 64 ants marched up the tree. 23 more joined them. Then 39 ants marched away carrying leaves. How many ants are left on the tree?

_____ ants

2. Monica counted 57 pennies in her bank. Her brother gave her 23 pennies. Her father gave her 15 more. How many pennies does Monica have now?

_____ pennies

Visual Thinking

3. Write a story problem for the picture.

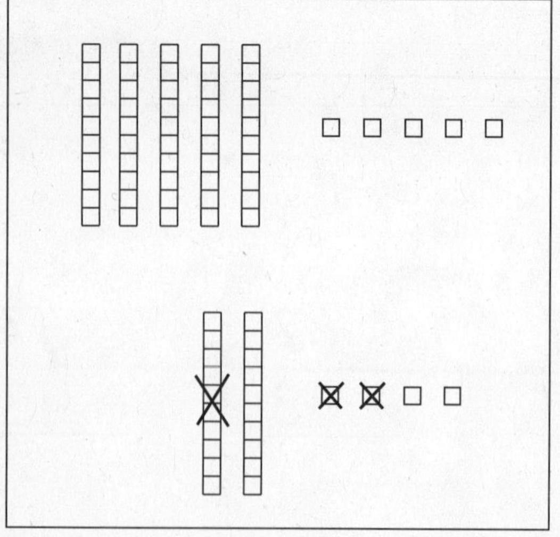

____

____

____

____

____

Notes for Home Your child drew pictures, wrote number sentences, and made up a story to solve problems.
Home Activity: Have your child write two number sentences for Exercise 3. (55 + 24 = 79 and 79 – 12 = 67)

Name ______________________________

Mixed Practice: Lessons 1–7

Subtract.

1. 6 tens − 4 tens   60 − 40

2. 9 tens − 7 tens   90 − 70

Use the chart to subtract.

3. 47 − 10 = ____

4. 36 − 30 = ____

5. 28 − 20 = ____

1	2	3	4	5	6	7	8	9	10
11	12	13	14	15	16	17	18	19	20
21	22	23	24	25	26	27	28	29	30
31	32	33	34	35	36	37	38	39	40
41	42	43	44	45	46	47	48	49	50

Problem Solving

Choose a way to solve the problem. Draw the place-value blocks or write a number sentence.

6. 25 people get on the bus. At the next stop, 8 get off and 4 get on. How many people are on the bus now? ____ people

Journal

7. Do you need to regroup to subtract? How do you know?

67 − 6   44 − 7

Notes for Home Your child practiced subtracting tens, using a hundred chart, and choosing a strategy to solve a problem. *Home Activity:* Have your child use a different strategy to solve Exercise 3.

Name ______________________________

Cumulative Review

Draw the clock hands. Write the ending time.

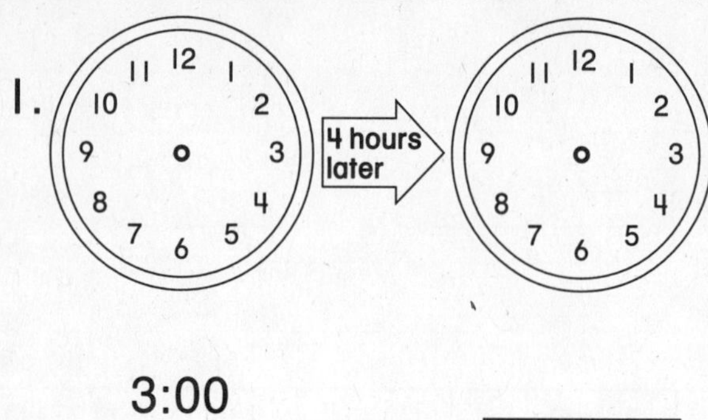

Problem Solving

Circle **add** or **subtract.** Write a number sentence. Solve.

3. 5 children are at the park. 7 more join them. How many children are at the park now?

   add **subtract**

   ____

   _____ children

4. 8 horses are running in the field. 3 run away. How many are left?

   add subtract

   ____

   _____ horses

Test Prep

Fill in ○ for the correct answer.
Add. Regroup if you need to.

5. $\begin{array}{r} 26 \\ +\ 35 \\ \hline \end{array}$ ○ 63 ○ 61 ○ 51 ○ 53

6. $\begin{array}{r} 57 \\ +\ 33 \\ \hline \end{array}$ ○ 80 ○ 90 ○ 89 ○ 70

7. $\begin{array}{r} 34 \\ +\ 54 \\ \hline \end{array}$ ○ 98 ○ 9 ○ 88 ○ 78

Notes for Home Your child reviewed telling time, addition and subtraction facts, and writing number sentences.
Home Activity: Ask your child to explain his or her answer for Exercise 4.

Name ______________________________

Practice 9-8

Explore Subtracting Two-Digit Numbers

Find 35 − 19.

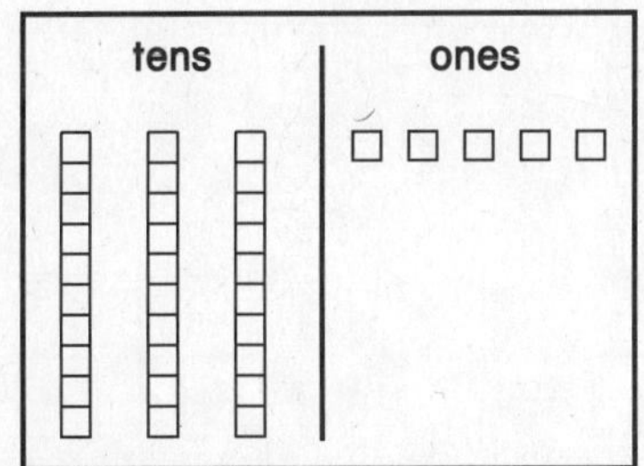

Take 35.

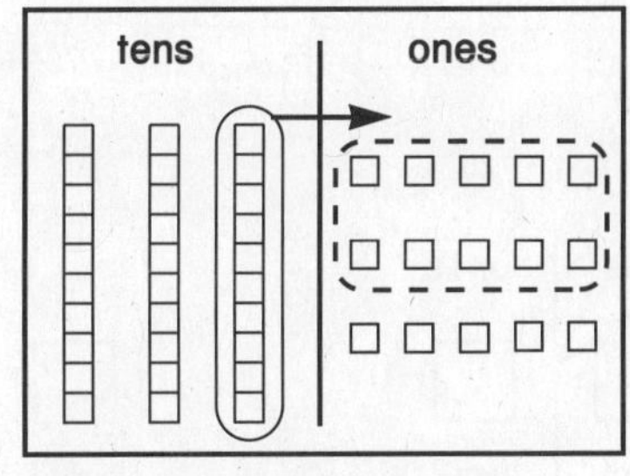

Regroup 1 ten as 10 ones.

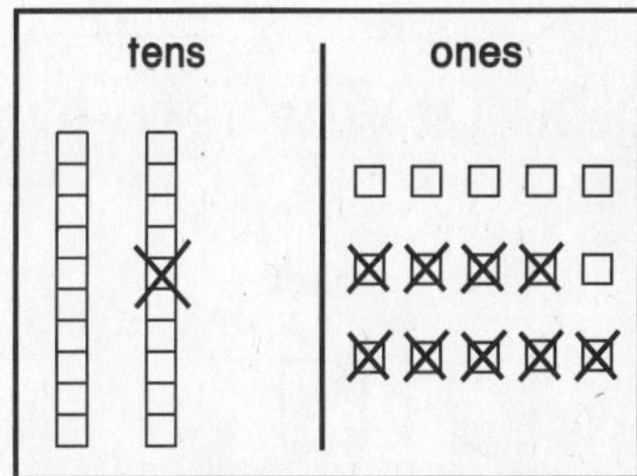

Subtract 19. Write the difference.

35 − 19 = 16

Use tens | ones, [ten rod], and [one cube] to subtract.

	Show this many.	Subtract this many.	Solve.
1.	33	27	33 − 27 = ____
2.	72	35	72 − 35 = ____
3.	48	19	48 − 19 = ____
4.	55	38	55 − 38 = ____
5.	17	9	17 − 9 = ____

Talk About It

Choose a problem on this page. Tell a classmate how you solved it.

Notes for Home Your child subtracted two-digit numbers with regrouping. *Home Activity:* Have your child use dried beans or macaroni to model Exercise 2.

Name ______________________________

Practice 9-9

Subtract Two- Digit Numbers With or Without Regrouping

Subtract. Use [tens | ones mat], [tens rod], and [ones cube].

Regroup if you need to.

1.

tens	ones
3	14
4	4
− 2	6
1	8

tens	ones
□	□
6	8
− 1	9

tens	ones
□	□
3	2
− 2	1

tens	ones
□	□
7	5
− 5	8

2.

tens	ones
□	□
5	1
− 3	4

tens	ones
□	□
8	3
− 7	1

tens	ones
□	□
2	6
− 1	8

tens	ones
□	□
9	1
− 6	2

Problem Solving Visual Thinking

3.

We started with this:	Now we have this:	Draw what was subtracted.
5 tens, 6 ones	3 tens, 9 ones	

Notes for Home Your child subtracted two-digit numbers with or without regrouping. *Home Activity:* Have your child tell you how to find the difference for 55 minus 37. (Regroup 1 ten for 10 ones. Subtract 7 ones from 15, and 3 tens from 4 tens; 18.)

 Use with pages 333–334.

Name ______________________________

Practice 9-10

Subtract Two-Digit Numbers

Subtract. Regroup if you need to.

1.

[5][17]					
67	58	33	45	16	27
− 48	− 26	− 16	− 37	− 11	− 19
19					

2.

50	48	33	85	10	72
− 16	− 39	− 14	− 67	− 7	− 54

Follow the rule. Subtract. Find the rule. Write the missing number.

3.

Subtract 19.	
70	
69	
50	
39	

4.

Subtract ______	
90	76
70	56
50	36
30	16

Problem Solving Critical Thinking

5. Fill in the missing numbers.

```
  [4][ ]
  [ ] 6
− 3 [ ]
  [ ] 8
```


Notes for Home Your child subtracted two-digit numbers. *Home Activity:* Have your child work through the problems in Exercise 3 with you.

Name ______________________________

Use Addition to Check Subtraction

Practice 9-11

Subtract. Write an addition problem to check.

1.
$$\begin{array}{r} 37 \\ -\ 19 \\ \hline 18 \end{array} \qquad \begin{array}{r} 18 \\ +\ 19 \\ \hline 37 \end{array}$$

$$\begin{array}{r} 53 \\ -\ 25 \\ \hline \end{array} \qquad \begin{array}{r} \square \\ +\ \square \\ \hline \square \end{array}$$

$$\begin{array}{r} 92 \\ -\ 38 \\ \hline \end{array} \qquad \begin{array}{r} \square \\ +\ \square \\ \hline \square \end{array}$$

2.
$$\begin{array}{r} 83 \\ -\ 43 \\ \hline \end{array} \qquad \begin{array}{r} \square \\ +\ \square \\ \hline \square \end{array}$$

$$\begin{array}{r} 37 \\ -\ 8 \\ \hline \end{array} \qquad \begin{array}{r} \square \\ +\ \square \\ \hline \square \end{array}$$

$$\begin{array}{r} 56 \\ -\ 28 \\ \hline \end{array} \qquad \begin{array}{r} \square \\ +\ \square \\ \hline \square \end{array}$$

3.
$$\begin{array}{r} 24 \\ -\ 13 \\ \hline \end{array} \qquad \begin{array}{r} \square \\ +\ \square \\ \hline \square \end{array}$$

$$\begin{array}{r} 45 \\ -\ 29 \\ \hline \end{array} \qquad \begin{array}{r} \square \\ +\ \square \\ \hline \square \end{array}$$

$$\begin{array}{r} 30 \\ -\ 10 \\ \hline \end{array} \qquad \begin{array}{r} \square \\ +\ \square \\ \hline \square \end{array}$$

Problem Solving Critical Thinking

4. Lisa did these subtraction problems. Use addition to check her work. Did she do both problems correctly? Explain.

$$\begin{array}{r} 87 \\ -\ 49 \\ \hline 38 \end{array} \qquad \begin{array}{r} 53 \\ -\ 26 \\ \hline 39 \end{array}$$

Notes for Home Your child used addition to check subtraction. *Home Activity:* Have your child explain how he or she solved Exercise 4

Name ______________________________

Practice 9-12

Subtract Money

Subtract.

1.
```
   4 14
   5̸ 4̸¢
 − 3 8¢
 ------
   1 6¢
```

$$81¢ - 63¢ \qquad 27¢ - 15¢ \qquad 95¢ - 75¢ \qquad 43¢ - 26¢$$

2. $32¢ - 4¢ \qquad 17¢ - 10¢ \qquad 66¢ - 57¢ \qquad 54¢ - 33¢ \qquad 99¢ - 65¢ \qquad 21¢ - 15¢$

Mixed Practice

Add or subtract.

3. $24 + 34 \qquad 48 - 26 \qquad 76¢ + 15¢ \qquad 57 - 49 \qquad 31¢ - 13¢ \qquad 65 + 27$

4. $18¢ - 4¢ \qquad 17 + 27 \qquad 52¢ - 33¢ \qquad 35 + 22 \qquad 63 + 9 \qquad 94¢ - 65¢$

Problem Solving

Solve.

5. 12 apples are in the basket.
8 children each take one.
How many apples are there now?

_____ apples

Notes for Home Your child solved addition and subtraction problems involving money. *Home Activity:* Ask your child to subtract 67¢ from 96¢. (29¢)

Name ______________________________

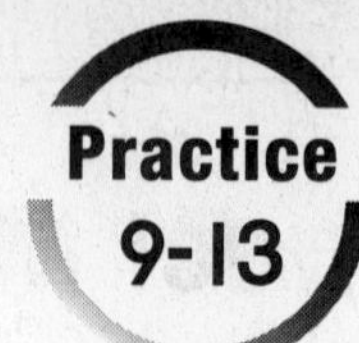

Problem Solving: Too Much Information

Solve. Cross out the information you do not need.

1. A swan can fly at about 55 miles in one hour. A crow can fly about 25 miles in one hour. An ostrich can run at about 31 miles per hour. How much faster can a swan fly than a crow?

   55
   − 25
   30 miles in one hour

2. The giant salamander is about 4 feet long. A python is the longest snake. It can grow to about 33 feet long. The giant squid can grow to about 56 feet long. How much longer is the python than the giant salamander?

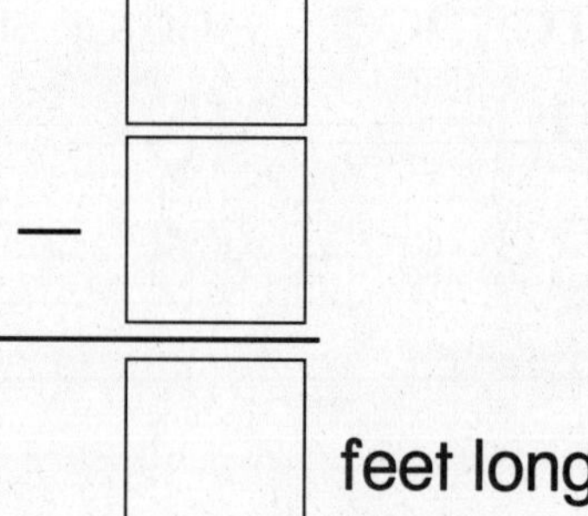

   feet longer

Journal

3. Write a math problem about playing baseball or basketball with too much information. Have a friend solve it.

____

____

____

Notes for Home Your child crossed out the information not needed to solve problems. *Home Activity:* Ask your child to explain his or her reasoning.

Name ______________________________

Practice
Chapter 9
B

Mixed Practice: Lessons 8–13

Subtract. Regroup if you need to.

1.

tens	ones
☐	☐
6	6
− 3	4

tens	ones
☐	☐
8	5
− 6	7

2.

$$\begin{array}{r} 52¢ \\ -\ 34¢ \\ \hline \end{array} \qquad \begin{array}{r} 17¢ \\ -\ 12¢ \\ \hline \end{array}$$

Subtract. Write an addition problem to check.

3.

$$\begin{array}{r} 44 \\ -\ 24 \\ \hline \end{array} \quad \begin{array}{r} \square \\ +\ \square \\ \hline \square \end{array} \qquad \begin{array}{r} 83 \\ -\ 65 \\ \hline \end{array} \quad \begin{array}{r} \square \\ +\ \square \\ \hline \square \end{array} \qquad \begin{array}{r} 26 \\ -\ 17 \\ \hline \end{array} \quad \begin{array}{r} \square \\ +\ \square \\ \hline \square \end{array}$$

Problem Solving

Solve. Cross out the information you do not need.

4. Maritza collected 57 stickers. It took her 6 months. Felipé collected 39 stickers. It took him 4 months. How many more stickers does Maritza have than Felipé?

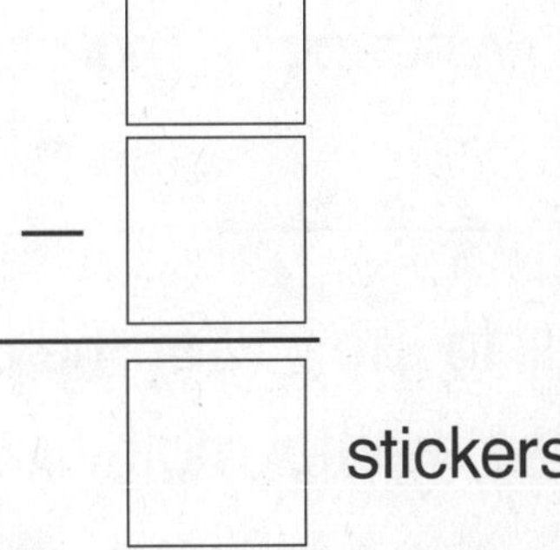

stickers

Journal

5. Write an addition problem to check this problem: 44 − 26 = 18. How do you know if it's correct? Explain.

Notes for Home Your child practiced subtracting two-digit numbers with and without regrouping, checking subtraction with addition, and crossing out information not needed in problems. *Home Activity:* Ask your child to explain his or her answers for Exercise 1.

Name ______________________

Practice
Chapters 1–9
B

Cumulative Review

Write the time.

1. 

_____ o'clock

_____ : _____

2. 

_____ : _____

3. 

_____ : _____

Problem Solving

Use the chart.

Marble colors	Tally	Totals
Green	~~////~~ ////	9
Orange	~~////~~ ~~////~~	10
Blue	~~////~~ /	6

4. How many more green marbles are there than blue marbles?

_____ more

5. What color marble is there fewest of in the jar? _____

Test Prep

Fill in the ○ for the correct answer.
Use mental math to add.

6. 46 + 40 = _____

56 ○ 67 ○ 86 ○ 76 ○

7. 23 + 60 = _____

73 ○ 83 ○ 63 ○ 93 ○

Notes for Home Your child reviewed telling time, solving problems, and adding. *Home Activity:* Ask your child to use mental math to add 33 and 60. (93)

Name ______________________________

Explore Hundreds

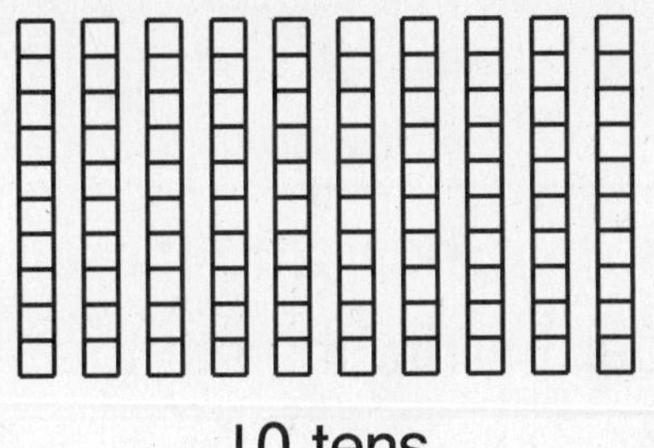

10 tens

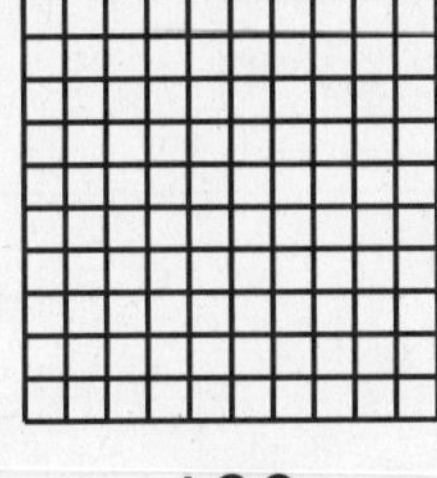

100

10 tens = 1 hundred

Write how many hundreds.
Write the number.

	How many hundreds?	Write the number.
1.	___ hundred	______
2.	___ hundreds	______
3.	___ hundreds	______
4.	___ hundreds	______
5.	___ hundreds	______
6.	___ hundreds	______

Journal

7. Write 2 things that you think might come packaged in hundreds.

Notes for Home Your child wrote how many hundreds and the number. *Home Activity:* Ask your child how many hundreds are in 700. (7 hundreds)

Name ________________________________

Identify Hundreds

Practice 10-2

Use 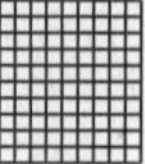 to complete the chart.

	Show this many. Write the number.	Show 200 less. Write the number.	Show 200 more. Write the number.
1.	200	0	400
2.	______	______	______
3.	______	______	______

Problem Solving Visual Thinking

4. Yani needs 800 cubes.
   Circle bags to show 800.

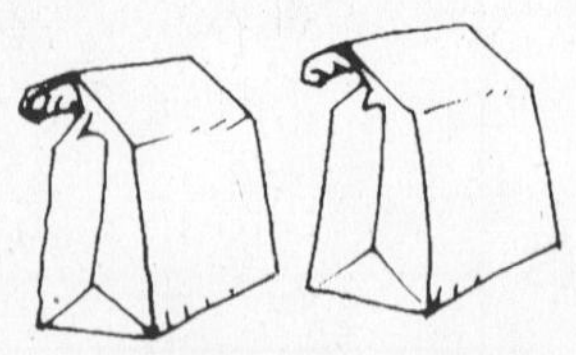
100 in each small bag

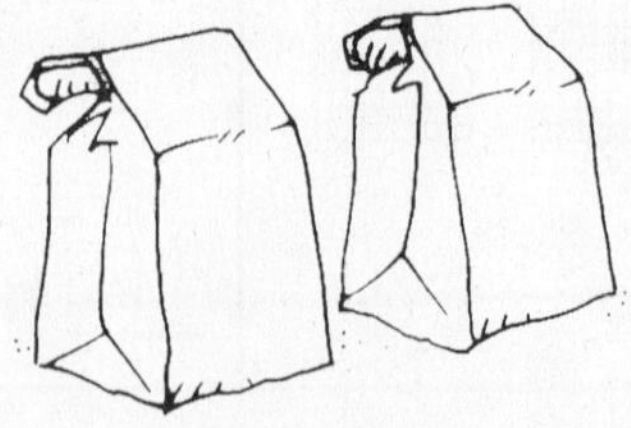
200 in each medium bag

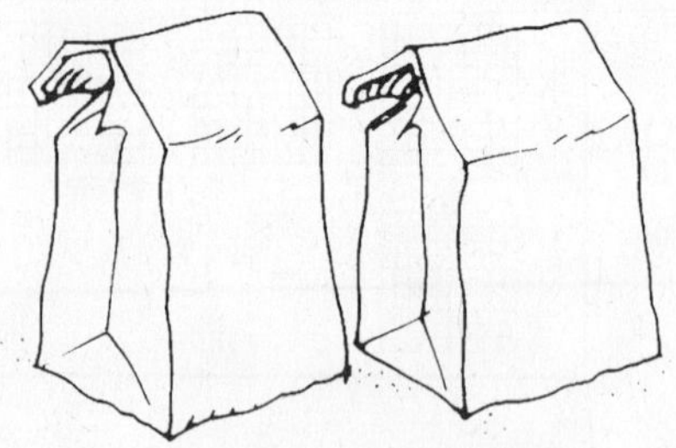
400 in each large bag

Notes for Home Your child practiced writing numbers for groups of 100. *Home Activity:* Ask your child to write the number that is 200 less than 900 and the number that is 200 more than 100. (700 and 300)

Name ______________________________

Practice 10-3

Write Three-Digit Numbers

Write how many hundreds, tens, and ones.
Write the number.

You can use | hundreds | tens | ones | and 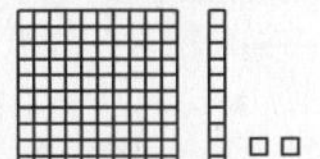 .

1. 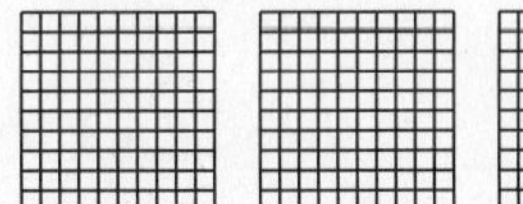

hundreds	tens	ones
3	0	5

______

2. 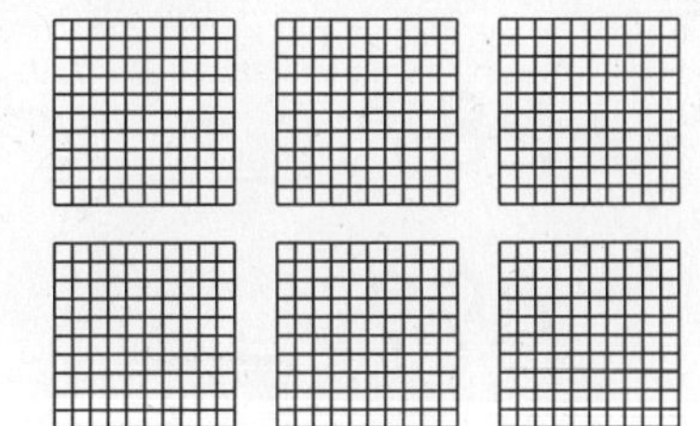

hundreds	tens	ones

______

Write your own. Choose your own number. Draw the ▦ ▯ ▫▫ .
Then write the number.

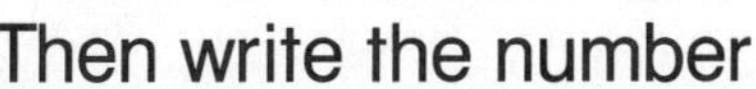

3.

hundreds	tens	ones

______

Problem Solving Patterns

Find each answer. What pattern do you see?

4. How many 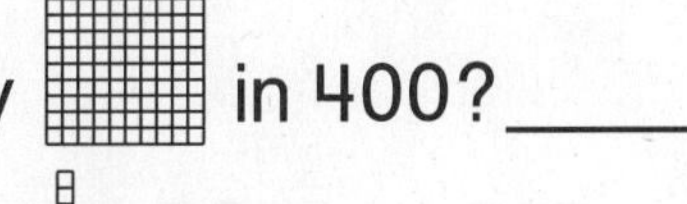 in 400? ______

How many ▯ in 400? ______

How many ▫▫ in 400? ______

5. How many 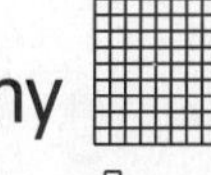 in 800? ______

How many ▯ in 800? ______

How many ▫▫ in 800? ______

Notes for Home Your child wrote three-digit numbers. *Home Activity:* Have your child look in a newspaper, magazine, or book for a three-digit number and tell you how many hundreds, tens, and ones are in the number. (Hint: Page numbers in books frequently run to three digit numbers.)

Name ______________________

Practice 10-4

Before, After, Between

Write the number that comes one before.

1. 154, 155 ______, 121 ______, 186
2. ______, 378 ______, 599 ______, 701
3. ______, 411 ______, 600 ______, 259

Write the number that comes one after.

4. 734, 735 551, ______ 287, ______
5. 414, ______ 880, ______ 699, ______
6. 108, ______ 348, ______ 99, ______

Write the number that comes between.

7. 214, 215, 216 589, ______, 591
8. 777, ______, 779 305, ______, 307
9. 880, ______, 882 98, ______, 100

Problem Solving

10. Write all the even numbers between 515 and 535.

516, 518, ______________________

____

Notes for Home Your child identified numbers that are one before, one after, and between other numbers. *Home Activity:* Pick 3 numbers between 100 and 500. For each, ask your child to say the number that comes one before it and the number that comes one after it.

Name ______________________________

Practice 10-5

Compare Numbers

Compare the numbers.
Write >, <, or =.

> is greater than
< is less than
= is equal to

1. 521 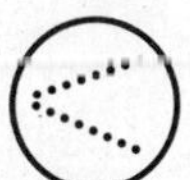 542   835 ◯ 816

2. 681  914   315 ◯ 315

3. 130 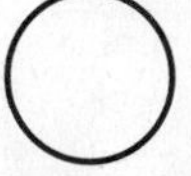 119   725 ◯ 735

Write your own numbers between
300 and 400 to make true statements.

4. 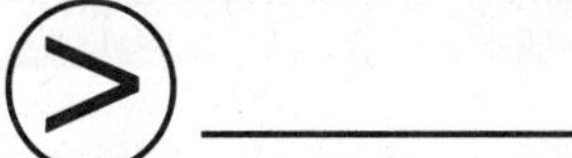 

5.  

6. 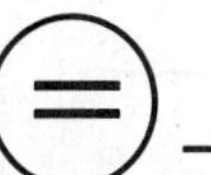 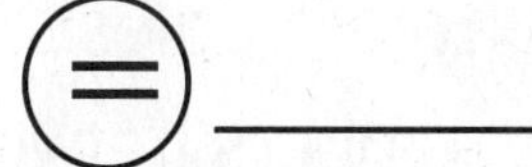

Problem Solving Critical Thinking

Solve the riddle.

7. I am a number less than 250 and greater than 245. I have 7 ones. What number am I?

____

8. I am an even number between 624 and 630. I have more than 6 ones. What number am I?

____

Notes for Home Your child compared numbers. *Home Activity:* Choose two numbers between 100 and 500. Ask your child to write the numbers and symbols to show "is greater than" and "is less than." (Possible choice and answers: 350 and 375; 350 < 375, 375 > 350.)

Name ______________________

Practice
10-6

Order Numbers

Write the numbers in order from least to greatest.

1. 225, 98, 187, 309 98, ____, ____, ____

2. 470, 417, 428, 459 ____, ____, ____, ____

Write the numbers in order from greatest to least.

3. 518, 377, 801, 495 801, ____, ____, ____

4. 350, 96, 606, 428 ____, ____, ____, ____

5. 770, 765, 707, 777 ____, ____, ____, ____

Write your own.

6. List four numbers in order from least to greatest. Choose numbers between 200 and 300. ____, ____, ____, ____

7. List four numbers in order from greatest to least. Choose numbers between 800 and 900. ____, ____, ____, ____

Problem Solving Estimation

8. These stacks of crayons will be sent to different schools. Draw lines to match each number to a stack. Then write the numbers in order from least to greatest.

264 216 288 240

____, ____, ____, ____

Notes for Home Your child put numbers in order. *Home Activity:* Ask your child where he or she would place a stack of 228 crayons in Exercise 8. (Between 216 and 240.)

Name ______________________________

Practice 10-7

Problem Solving:
Group Decision Making

Work with your group to solve the problem.

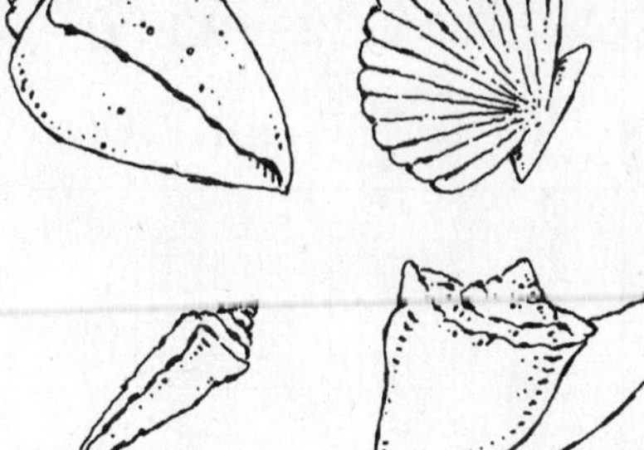

1. Roy and Reba are buying shells to make jewelry. They need 60 shells in all for their projects. Roy buys 12 shells. Reba buys 18 shells. How many more shells do they need to buy?

Understand What does the problem ask? How many more shells do Roy and Reba need to buy?

Plan How can you solve the problem? ______________________________

____

Solve Solve the problem. ______________________________

____

Look Back Check your work. ______________________________

____

Write your own.

2. Work as a group to write a problem for another group to solve.

____

____

Notes for Home Your child used the Problem Solving Guide. *Home Activity:* Ask your child what way his or her group used to find, and then check, the answer to the problem.

Name ______________________

Mixed Practice: Lessons 1–7

Write 100 less and 100 more. You can use ▦.

	Show this many. Write the number.	Show 100 less. Write the number.	Show 100 more. Write the number.
1.	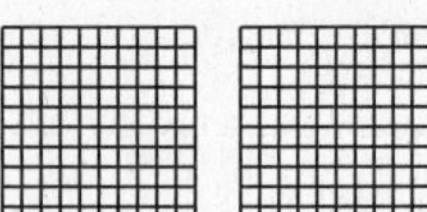 ______	______	______

Write how many hundreds, tens, and ones. Then write the number.

2. 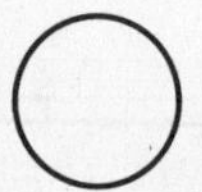 

hundreds	tens	ones

______

Write the number one before, one after, or between.

3. ______, 148 589, ______ 399, ______, 401

Compare. Write >, <, or =.

4. 380 ◯ 320 540 ◯ 540 793 ◯ 801

Problem Solving

Solve. Use the Problem Solving Guide to help.

5. Sabrina brought a box of 200 buttons for a project. Later she brought a box of 500 buttons. She used 190 buttons. How many buttons does she have now? ______ buttons

Notes for Home Your child practiced writing and comparing three-digit numbers. *Home Activity:* Ask your child what page in a book comes before and after page 381. (380 and 382)

Name ____________________

Practice
Chapters 1–10
A

Cumulative Review

Count the money.

Write the total amount.

1.

______

Problem Solving

Use the graph to answer the questions.

Coin Collections	
Tao	O O O
Jin	O O
Lee	O O O O
Each O means 10 coins.	

2. How many more coins does Tao have than Jin?

   ______ coins

3. How many coins in all do Tao, Jin, and Lee have?

   ______ coins

Test Prep

Fill in the ○ for the correct answer.

Subtract.

4. $80 - 45$

   45 ○ 35 ○ 65 ○ 25 ○

5. $92 - 60$

   30 ○ 32 ○ 20 ○ 22 ○

Notes for Home Your child reviewed counting money, using a graph to solve problems, and subtracting. *Home Activity:* Ask your child to look at the graph and tell how many fewer coins Jin has than Lee. (20 fewer coins)

Name ______________________

Add and Subtract Mentally

Practice 10-8

Add or subtract. Use mental math.

1. 60 + 30 = 90   400 + 200   300 + 100   50 + 20   300 + 500

$$\begin{array}{r}60\\+30\\\hline 90\end{array}\quad\begin{array}{r}400\\+200\\\hline\end{array}\quad\begin{array}{r}300\\+100\\\hline\end{array}\quad\begin{array}{r}50\\+20\\\hline\end{array}\quad\begin{array}{r}300\\+500\\\hline\end{array}$$

2.

$$\begin{array}{r}70\\-10\\\hline\end{array}\quad\begin{array}{r}800\\-300\\\hline\end{array}\quad\begin{array}{r}600\\-200\\\hline\end{array}\quad\begin{array}{r}80\\-30\\\hline\end{array}\quad\begin{array}{r}40\\-30\\\hline\end{array}$$

Follow the rule.

3.

Add 100	
200	
500	
100	
600	

4.

Subtract 10	
340	
410	
790	
950	

5.

Add 30	
800	
620	
270	
440	

Problem Solving Patterns

Add or subtract. What patterns do you see?

6.

$$\begin{array}{r}3\\+6\\\hline\end{array}\quad\begin{array}{r}33\\+66\\\hline\end{array}\quad\begin{array}{r}333\\+666\\\hline\end{array}$$

7.

$$\begin{array}{r}8\\-2\\\hline\end{array}\quad\begin{array}{r}88\\-22\\\hline\end{array}\quad\begin{array}{r}888\\-222\\\hline\end{array}$$

Notes for Home Your child added and subtracted using mental math. *Home Activity:* Ask your child to explain how to use mental math to subtract 500 – 200. (5 – 2 = 3; 500 – 200 = 300)

Name ______________________________

Add Three-Digit Numbers

Practice 10-9

Show each number. Add.

You can use [hundreds | tens | ones] and [blocks].

1.

hundreds	tens	ones
2	4	6
+ 2	1	3
4	5	9

hundreds	tens	ones
3	5	1
+ 1	0	7

hundreds	tens	ones
6	0	4
+ 2	6	3

2.

$$\begin{array}{r} 231 \\ +\ 137 \\ \hline \end{array} \quad \begin{array}{r} 125 \\ +\ 64 \\ \hline \end{array} \quad \begin{array}{r} 726 \\ +\ 203 \\ \hline \end{array} \quad \begin{array}{r} 205 \\ +\ 381 \\ \hline \end{array} \quad \begin{array}{r} 523 \\ +\ 263 \\ \hline \end{array}$$

3.

$$\begin{array}{r} 146 \\ +\ 132 \\ \hline \end{array} \quad \begin{array}{r} 219 \\ +\ 260 \\ \hline \end{array} \quad \begin{array}{r} 307 \\ +\ 92 \\ \hline \end{array} \quad \begin{array}{r} 115 \\ +\ 151 \\ \hline \end{array} \quad \begin{array}{r} 430 \\ +\ 305 \\ \hline \end{array}$$

Problem Solving

4. Fill in the missing numbers.

hundreds	tens	ones
☐	2	☐
+ 3	☐	5
4	7	9

hundreds	tens	ones
4	☐	5
+ ☐	7	☐
5	9	5

hundreds	tens	ones
☐	6	☐
+ 3	☐	4
8	7	6

Notes for Home Your child added three-digit numbers. *Home Activity:* Ask your child to tell you what the missing three-digit number is in 352 + ___ = 586. (234)

Name ______________________________

Add Three-Digit Numbers With or Without Regrouping

Add. Regroup if you need to.

You can use 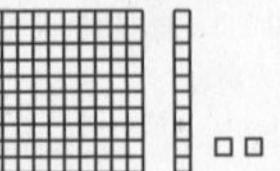 and ▦ ▯ ▫▫.

1.

hundreds	tens	ones
□	□	
3	2	5
+ 2	4	7
5	7	2

hundreds	tens	ones
□	□	
4	6	8
+ 3	0	7

hundreds	tens	ones
□	□	
6	7	3
+ 2	7	5

2.

335	619	380	155	518
+ 48	+ 124	+ 65	+ 793	+ 291

3.

258	775	406	670	189
+ 327	+ 19	+ 285	+ 86	+ 150

Problem Solving

Solve.

4. Jose made 125 cat pins for the craft fair. Martina made 148 dog pins. How many pet pins did they make in all?

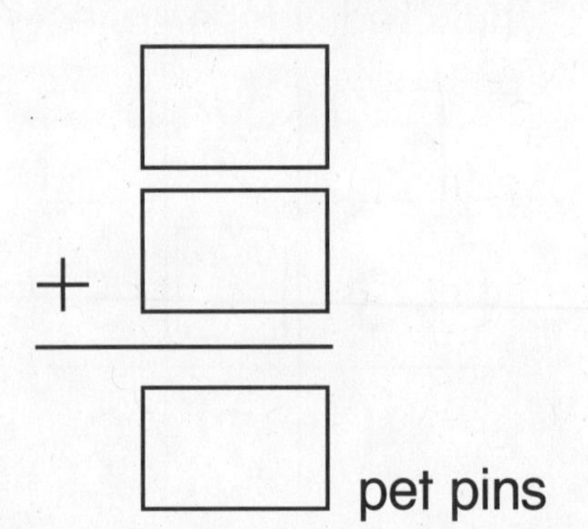

Notes for Home Your child added with and without regrouping. *Home Activity:* Pick a number between 100 and 500. Have your child pick another number between 100 and 500. Ask your child to tell you whether he or she must regroup to add the two numbers. (Examples: 326, 142, no; 326, 184, yes.)

Name ______________________

Practice 10-11

Subtract Three-Digit Numbers

Show each number. Subtract.

You can use

hundreds	tens	ones

and 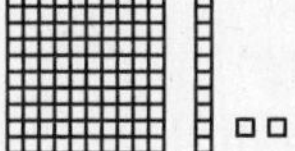.

1.

hundreds	tens	ones
6	4	8
− 3	1	5
3	3	3

hundreds	tens	ones
8	9	5
− 1	0	2

hundreds	tens	ones
7	4	6
− 6	1	5

2. $745 - 234$ $386 - 62$ $942 - 301$ $555 - 43$ $489 - 115$

3. $678 - 26$ $896 - 143$ $357 - 245$ $779 - 320$ $935 - 20$

Write a math story.

4. Use these numbers to write a math story. Then solve.

$745 - 234$

____

____

____

____

____

Notes for Home Your child subtracted three-digit numbers. *Home Activity:* Ask your child to estimate the answer then check the estimate on paper for the problem 678 – 214. (Estimates will vary. Sample estimate is 700 – 200, or 500. Answer is 464.)

Name ______________________________

Subtract Three-Digit Numbers With or Without Regrouping

Subtract. Regroup if you need to.

You can use [hundreds | tens | ones] and [place-value blocks].

1.

hundreds	tens	ones
	3	12
6	~~4~~	~~2~~
−	2	8
6	1	4

hundreds	tens	ones
4	2	9
− 1	5	6

hundreds	tens	ones
8	4	0
− 4	1	5

2. $562 - 147$ $864 - 329$ $318 - 42$ $624 - 273$ $295 - 76$

3. $480 - 126$ $709 - 225$ $593 - 328$ $854 - 309$ $666 - 107$

Problem Solving Critical Thinking

4. You need to regroup twice.
What could the missing numbers be?

hundreds	tens	ones
6	☐	8
− 4	5	☐

Notes for Home Your child subtracted three-digit numbers with regrouping. *Home Activity:* Ask your child to write a subtraction problem that needs regrouping and a problem that does not need regrouping. Then have him or her show you how to solve the problems.

Name ______________________

Practice 10-13

Problem Solving:
Use Data from a Picture

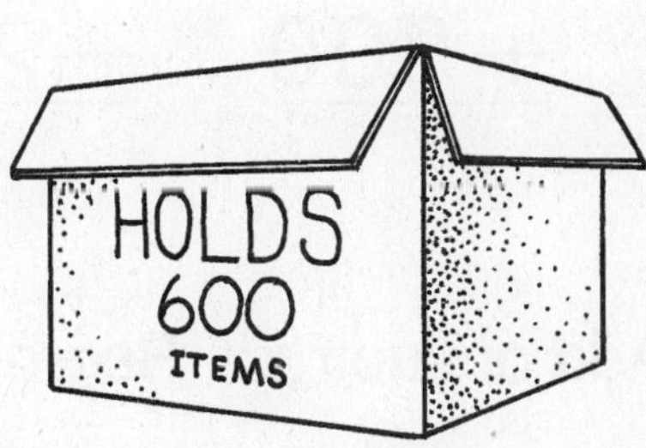

1. Kris puts the tub of stones in the box. What else can he put in?

   ____

2. Sarah puts 570 items in the box. What did she put in?

   ____

3. Leon put the buttons in the box. What else can he put in?

   ____

4. Lana put 500 items in the box. What did she put in?

   ____

5. Dana puts 540 items in the box. What did she put in?

   ____

Critical Thinking

6. Are there any 3 tubs that could be put in the box together? Explain your answer.

   ____

   ____

Notes for Home Your child used the numbers in the picture to solve problems. *Home Activity:* Ask your child which two tubs together hold the least number of items. (Shells and beads)

Name ______________________________

Practice
Chapter 10
B

Mixed Practice: Lessons 8–13

Add or subtract. Use mental math.

1.

400	700	60	800	55
+ 300	+ 200	− 40	− 200	+ 33

Add or subtract. Regroup if you need to.

2.

463	748	537	638	370
+ 26	− 153	+ 281	− 18	+ 426

Problem Solving

Use the picture to answer the questions.

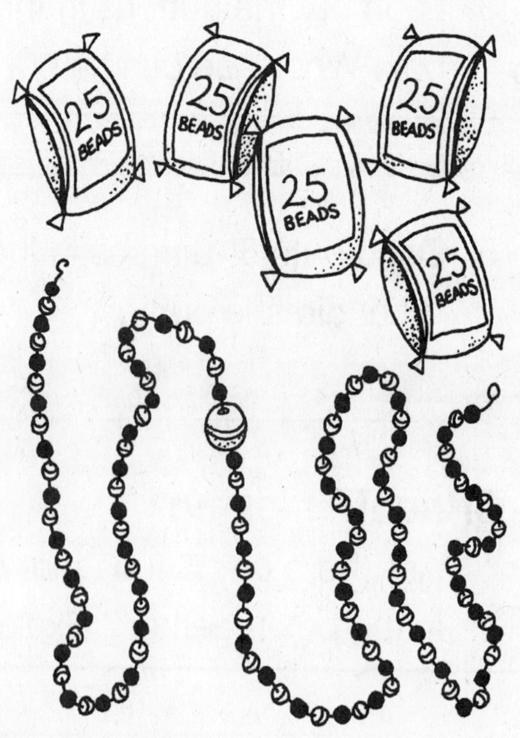

3. Doreen needs 125 beads to make a Navaho necklace. How many bags of beads does she need?

   ______ bags of beads

4. Donny has 2 bags of beads. How many more bags of beads does he need to make a Navaho necklace?

   ______ bags of beads

Journal

5. How did the pictures help you answer the problems?

Notes for Home Your child practiced the skills and concepts from this section. *Home Activity:* Ask your child how many bags of beads would be needed if it takes 150 beads to make a different necklace. (6 bags of beads)

Name ______________________________

Practice
Chapters 1–10
B

Cumulative Review

Write the number of tens and ones.

Then write the number.

1.

______ tens and ______ ones

______

2. 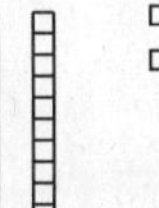

______ tens and ______ ones

______

Does the activity take less or more than one minute?

Circle **less** or **more**.

3. eating dinner

less more

4. closing a door

less more

5. sneezing

less more

6. cleaning your room

less more

Test Prep

Fill in the ○ for the correct answer.

Add.

7. 46¢ + 23¢

69¢ ○ 79¢ ○ 13¢ ○ 23¢ ○

8. 38¢ + 15¢

43¢ ○ 53¢ ○ 23¢ ○ 48¢ ○

Notes for Home Your child reviewed identifying and writing tens and ones, estimating if activities take more or less than one minute, and adding amounts of money. *Home Activity:* Ask your child to tell you the fewest number of coins that make 43¢. (1 quarter, 1 dime, 1 nickel, 3 pennies)

Name ______________________________

Practice 11-1

Explore Nonstandard Units

Estimate the lengths. Use Snap Cubes to measure. Write the numbers.

1.

Estimate: about 3 Snap Cubes

Measure: about ______ Snap Cubes

2.

Estimate: about ______ Snap Cubes

Measure: about ______ Snap Cubes

3.

Estimate: about ______ Snap Cubes

Measure: about ______ Snap Cubes

Problem Solving Critical Thinking

4. Milita measured the length of her arm.
First she measured with connecting cubes.
Then she measured with new crayons.
Did Milita need more cubes or more crayons?

____

Notes for Home Your child estimated and measured the lengths of objects using cubes. *Home Activity:* Ask your child to use a spoon to measure the length of a table in your home.

 Use with pages 401–402.

Name ______________________________

Inches and Feet

Estimate about how many inches.

Measure with your inch ruler.

1. What to Measure	Estimate	Measurement
width of your hand	about ____ inches	about ____ inches

Estimate about how many feet.

Measure with your yardstick.

2. What to Measure	Estimate	Measurement
width of a door	about ____ inches	about ____ inches

Write your own.

Draw or write what you will measure.

Use inches or feet to measure.

3. What to Measure	Estimate	Measurement
	about ____	about ____

Problem Solving Visual Thinking

4. Look at the two ant paths.
   Circle the path you think is longer.
   Explain. You can use string to check.

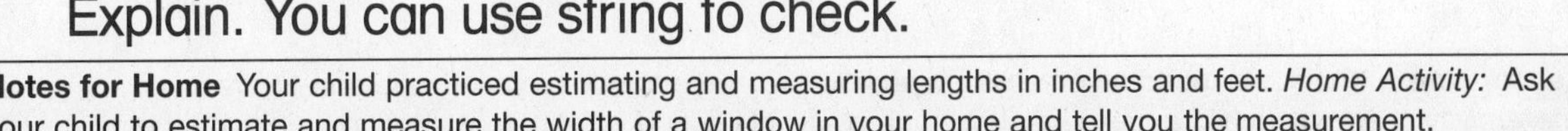

Notes for Home Your child practiced estimating and measuring lengths in inches and feet. *Home Activity:* Ask your child to estimate and measure the width of a window in your home and tell you the measurement.

Name ____________________

Practice 11-3

Inches, Feet, and Yards

Complete the chart.

	Estimate. Find an object about this long.	Write or draw the object.	Measure length to check.
1.	about 2 inches		about ______
2.	about 2 feet		about ______
3.	about 2 yards		about ______

Problem Solving Estimation

Circle the best estimate of length.

4. 

about 1 inch

about 1 foot

about 1 yard

5. 

about 1 inch

about 1 foot

about 1 yard

6. 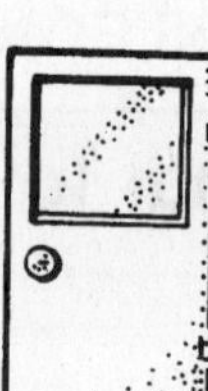

about 1 inch

about 1 foot

about 1 yard

Notes for Home Your child found and measured objects that were about 1 inch, 1 foot, and 1 yard long. *Home Activity:* Give your child a measurement, such as 3 inches, and have him or her find an object around home that is about that long.

Name ______________________________

Centimeters and Meters

Estimate about how many meters.

Measure with a meter stick.

	What to Measure	Estimate	Measure
1.	width of a window	about ______ meters	about ______ meters
2.	height of a door	about ______ meters	about ______ meters
3.	distance from the front wall of your classroom to the rear wall	about ______ meters	about ______ meters

Mental Math

4. Solve.

Jon is 132 centimeters tall. Jennie is 128 centimeters tall.

How much taller is Jon?

______ centimeters taller

Notes for Home Your child estimated and measured length and height in meters. *Home Activity:* Ask your child to estimate the width of a room in your home in meters.

Name ______________________________

Perimeter

1. Mark an X on the shape that you estimate has the greatest perimeter. Measure the lengths of the sides. Add to find the perimeter. Circle the shape with the greatest perimeter.

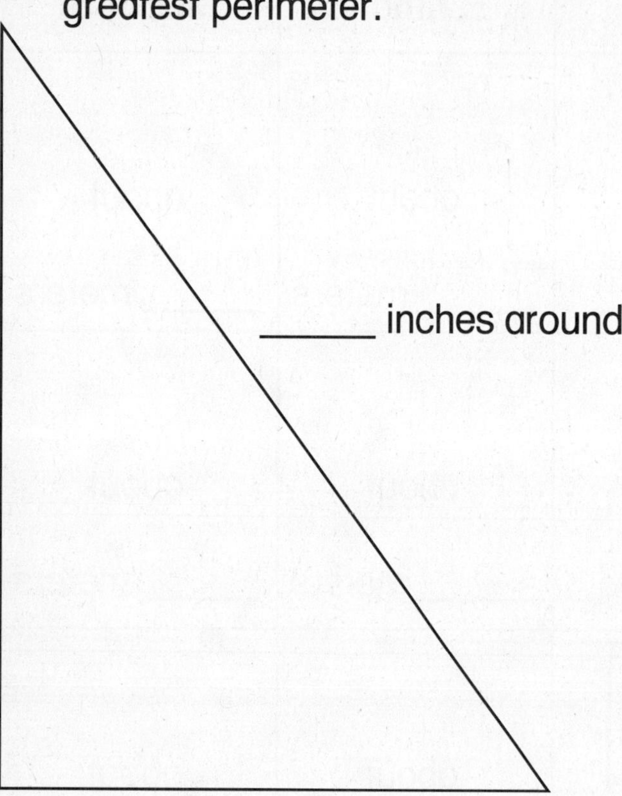

______ inches around

______ inches around

______ inches around

Problem Solving Visual Thinking

2. Do not measure. Which has the greater perimeter, the square or the rectangle. How do you know?

____

____

Notes for Home Your child practiced finding the perimeter of different shapes and objects. *Home Activity:* Give your child a book or magazine and ask him or her to find the perimeter.

Name ______________________________

Practice 11-6

Explore Area

Estimate how many [Snap Cube] will cover the shape.
Draw square units to show what you did.

1. Estimate: _____ Snap Cubes

   Measure: _____ square units

2. Estimate: _____ Snap Cubes

   Measure: _____ square units

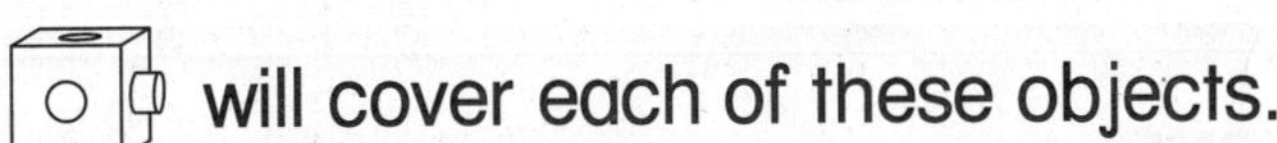

Estimate how many [Snap Cube] will cover each of these objects.

Use [Snap Cube] to check your estimate.

3. top of a chalkboard eraser

   Estimate: _____ Snap Cubes

   Measure: _____ Snap Cubes

4. this piece of paper

   Estimate: _____ Snap Cubes

   Measure: _____ Snap Cubes

Problem Solving Critical Thinking

5. Each side of the large square is twice as long as a side of the small square. Which would you need fewer of to cover the top of your desk? Why? Circle your answer. ______________________________

____

Notes for Home Your child practiced using Snap Cubes to cover the area of different shapes.
Home Activity: Ask your child to tell you how he or she would use a Snap Cube to find the area of a table top.

Name ______________________________

Practice
11-7

Problem Solving:
Use Objects

Use centimeter cubes to make each shape.
Color the grid to show the shape.

1. Make a rectangle that covers 8 square units inside and has a perimeter of 12 units around the outside.

2. Make a rectangle that covers 14 square units inside and has a perimeter of 18 units around the outside.

Write your own.

3. Draw your own shape.
Tell about your shape.

My shape:
is ____________________.
has a perimeter of _____ units.
has _____ square units inside.

Journal

4. Make some shapes that have the same number of square units inside, but different perimeters. Draw the shapes. Tell about them.

Notes for Home Your child solved problems involving area and perimeter. *Home Activity:* Work with your child to make a chart that shows the perimeters of different rectangles that have an area of 16 square units. You may find something interesting about the one with the smallest perimeter.

Name ______________________________

Practice
Chapter 11
A

Mixed Practice: Lessons 1–7

Estimate the length. Measure with a centimeter ruler.

1. Estimate: about _____ centimeters long

   Measure: about _____ centimeters long

Estimate the perimeter and area. Measure with an inch ruler and use ▢ to cover the shape.

2. Perimeter

   Estimate: _____ inches around

   Measure: _____ inches around

3. Area

   Estimate: _____ square units

   Measure: _____ square units

Problem Solving

Draw a different shape with the same area.

4. Area: _____ square units

   Perimeter: _____ units

5. Area: _____ square units

   Perimeter: _____ units

Journal

6. Draw a shape. Label it A. Draw another shape with the same area as A but a different perimeter. Draw another shape with the same perimeter as A but a different area.

Notes for Home Your child practiced estimating and measuring length, perimeter, and area. *Home Activity:* Have your child find the perimeter of an object such as a book or magazine. Then have him or her find another object in your home with a greater perimeter.

Name ______________________________

Cumulative Review

Add

1.

47	60	72	14	28	53
+ 24	+ 38	+ 8	+ 13	+ 35	+ 24

Write how many hundreds, tens, and ones.
Then write the number.

2. 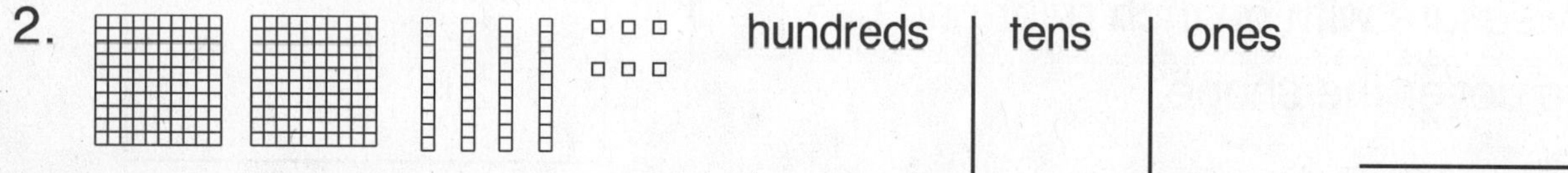

hundreds	tens	ones

______

Problem Solving

Solve.

3. Penny packs 16 cartons with soda crackers. Then she packs 14 cartons with cheese crackers. How many cartons did Penny pack?

______ cartons

4. Pete packs 28 bags of peppers in the morning. He packs 32 bags in the afternoon. How many bags did Pete pack?

______ bags

Test Prep

Fill in the ○ for the correct answer.

5. Choose the number that comes just before 749.

○ 750 ○ 748 ○ 794

6. Choose the number that comes just after 519.

○ 518 ○ 529 ○ 520

Notes for Home Your child reviewed 2-digit addition, writing large numbers, and using addition to solve problems. *Home Activity:* Ask your child to make up an addition problem. Then have him or her tell you how to solve it and give the sum.

Name ______________________________

Explore One Pound

Is each object **heavier than**, **lighter than**, or **about** 1 pound? Estimate. Then use a pound weight to check. Complete the chart.

	Object	Estimate	Measure
1.		______ 1 pound	______ 1 pound
2.	TELEPHONE	______ 1 pound	______ 1 pound
3.		______ 1 pound	______ 1 pound
4.		______ 1 pound	______ 1 pound
5.	JUICE	______ 1 pound	______ 1 pound

Tell a Math Story

6. Write a math story about something that is heavier than a pound and something that is lighter than a pound.

Notes for Home Your child estimated whether objects weigh more or less than 1 pound. *Home Activity:* Visit a food store with your child and check the labels on different foods. Explain that 16 oz (ounces) is a pound, anything over 16 oz is heavier than a pound and anything under 16 oz is lighter than a pound. Have him or her make lists of the foods over, about, or under a pound.

Name ______________________________

Practice 11-9

Kilograms

1. Circle in red the objects that are lighter than 1 kilogram
2. Circle in blue the objects that are heavier than 1 kilogram.

Write your own. Choose an object. Is your object lighter or heavier than 1 kilogram?

My object:__________ __________ than a kilogram

Problem Solving Critical Thinking

3. Which weighs more, a football or a bowling ball? Explain. _______

____

Notes for Home Your child identified objects that are lighter or heavier than 1 kilogram. *Home Activity:* Ask your child to make a list of 5 objects that are heavier than a kilogram and 5 objects that are lighter than a kilogram. (A kilogram is about 2 1/5 pounds.)

Name ______________________________

Practice 11-10

Cups, Pints, and Quarts

Solve.

1. Larry has 3 pints of milk. Color the number of cups he could fill.

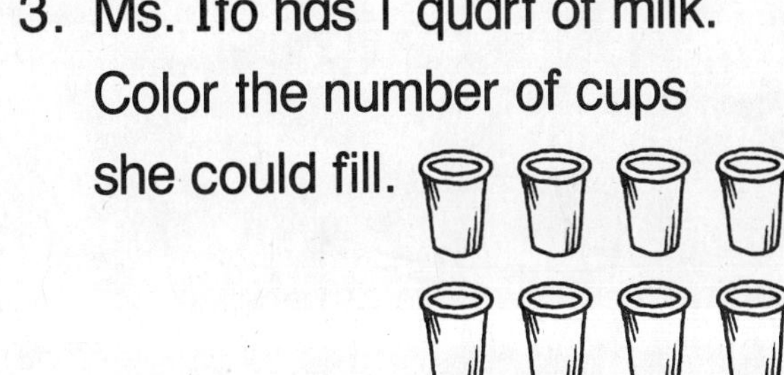

2. Shelly buys 2 pints of milk. Color the number of cups she could fill.

3. Ms. Ito has 1 quart of milk. Color the number of cups she could fill.

4. Indra wants 6 pints of juice. Color the number of quarts that hold the same amount.

5. Sani wants 3 quarts of juice. Color the number of pints that hold the same amount.

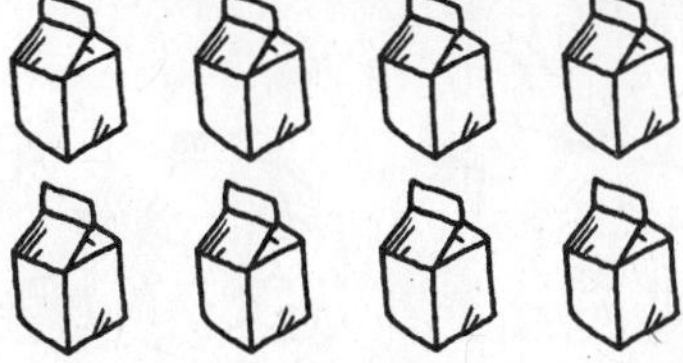

Problem Solving Visual Thinking

6. Draw cups to solve.
Raul has 3 quarts of juice.
Rita has 10 cups of juice. Who has more?

_______________ has more.

Notes for Home Your child solved problems about cups, pints, and quarts. *Home Activity:* Give your child a measuring cup and some empty containers. Have him or her find the number of cups that each container can hold.

Name ______________________________

Liters

Practice 11-11

1. Which things hold less than one liter?
   Circle them.

2. Which things hold more than one liter?
   Mark an X on them.

Mental Math

3. A keg holds eight liters of cider.
   How many liters will ten kegs hold?

   ______ liters

Notes for Home Your child identified containers that hold more or less than one liter. *Home Activity:* When you visit a grocery store, ask your child to identify containers that hold more than, less than, and about one liter.

Name ________________________________

Problem Solving:
Group Decision Making

Make your own recipe for punch.
You need to make 40 cups.

1. Write your recipe on this card.
   Write a name for your punch.

Our Recipe: ________________________	
How much?	What kind of juice?

Answer these questions about your punch recipe.

2. How many cups of punch does your recipe make? 40
3. How many pints of punch does your recipe make? ______
4. How many quarts of punch does your recipe make? ______

Journal

5. Write a punch recipe for your family.
   Make enough for each person to have 2 cups.

Notes for Home Your child explored making decisions with a group to create recipes. *Home Activity:* Ask your child to tell you how many cups of each kind of juice would be needed in his or her family recipe if each member wanted 4 cups. (Double each ingredient.)

Name ______________________________

Practice 11-13

Temperature

Color to show the temperature.

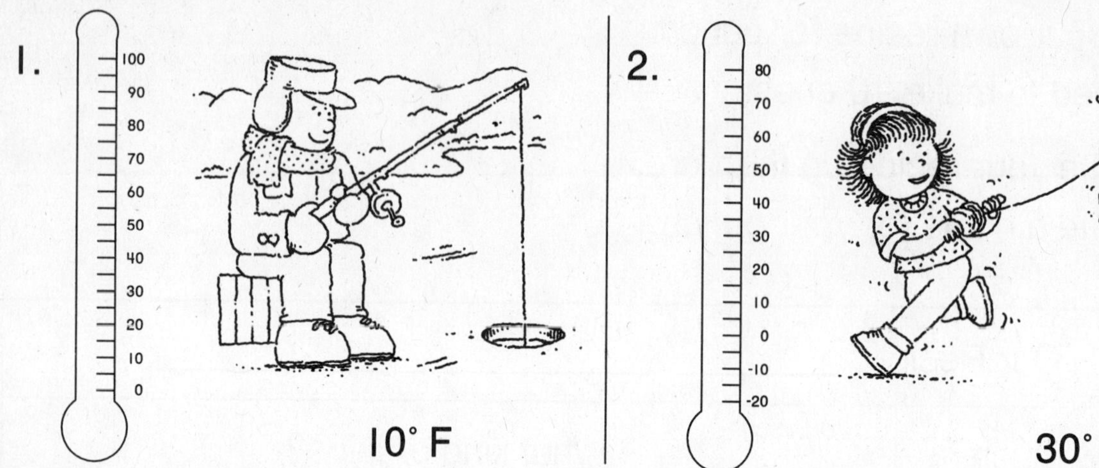

Write your own.

Choose and write a temperature. Color in the thermometer.

Draw a picture to show an activity you might do at that temperature.

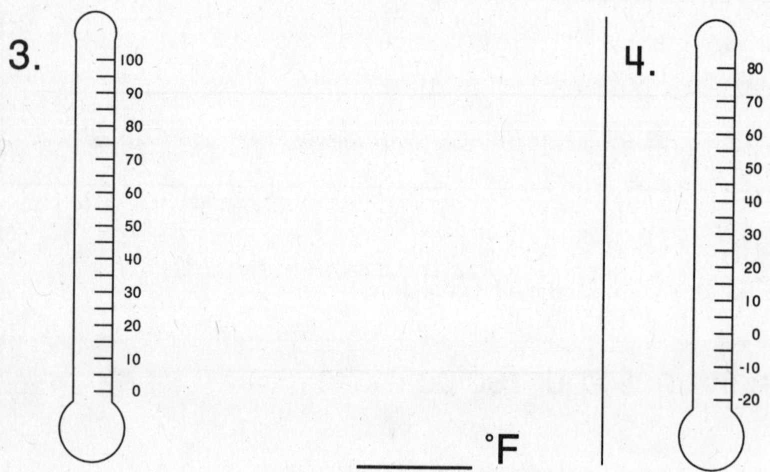

Problem Solving Critical Thinking

5. It is 20° Celsius outside today. You must walk to school. Should you wear a heavy coat or just a light sweater? Why?

Notes for Home Your child practiced showing different temperatures on thermometers. *Home Activity:* Ask your child when the temperature in Celsius and Fahrenheit will be cool enough outside for you to want to wear a coat. (At about 50° Fahrenheit and 10° Celsius, you might want to wear a coat, or at least a sweater, outside.)

Name ________________________________

Mixed Practice: Lessons 8–13

1. Color to show the temperature.

86° F

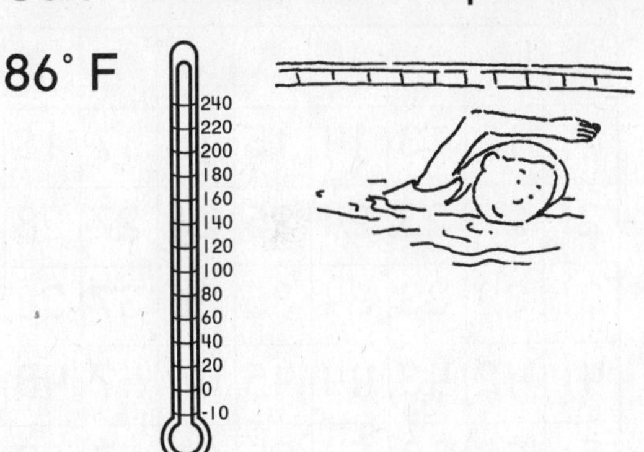

2° F

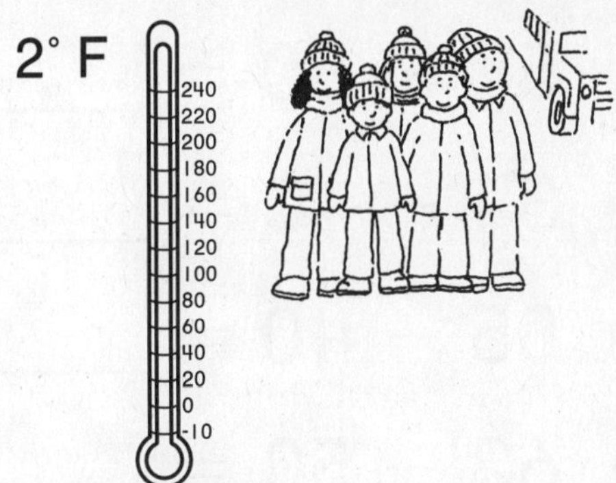

2. Is the pencil heavier or lighter than 1 pound? Write **heavier** or **lighter.**

   A pencil is ______________

3. Is the TV heavier or lighter than 1 kilogram? Write **heavier** or **lighter.**

   A TV is ______________

Problem Solving

Solve.

PUNCH

4 pints of grape juice
2 quarts of apple juice
8 cups of lemonade

4. You need to make 2 cups of punch for each of 10 party guests. Do you have enough? Circle **yes** or **no.**

   yes no

5. Which juice do you need more of in this recipe?

   ____

Journal

6. Keep track of the **temperature** at the same time each evening. Write about what you find.

Notes for Home Your child practiced finding temperatures, the weights of objects using kilograms and pounds, and amounts of liquids. *Home Activity:* Ask your child to estimate how much different objects around the home weigh. Weigh each object and compare the result with the estimate.

Name ______________________

Cumulative Review

Use the hundred chart to subtract.

1. 58 − 30 = ____
2. 34 − 10 = ____
3. 85 − 40 = ____
4. 62 − 50 = ____
5. 42 − 40 = ____
6. 98 − 60 = ____

1	2	3	4	5	6	7	8	9	10
11	12	13	14	15	16	17	18	19	20
21	22	23	24	25	26	27	28	29	30
31	32	33	34	35	36	37	38	39	40
41	42	43	44	45	46	47	48	49	50
51	52	53	54	55	56	57	58	59	60
61	62	63	64	65	66	67	68	69	70
71	72	73	74	75	76	77	78	79	80
81	82	83	84	85	86	87	88	89	90
91	92	93	94	95	96	97	98	99	100

Problem Solving

Write each number sentence. Solve.

7. 26 pumpkins are on the wagon.
8 more pumpkins are loaded on. ____________ pumpkins

At the first store, 10 pumpkins are unloaded. How many pumpkins are on the wagon now? ____________ pumpkins

Test Prep

Fill in the ○ for the correct answer.

8. $418 + 152$

○ 266
○ 562
○ 560
○ 570

9. $256 + 183$

○ 439
○ 336
○ 339
○ 133

Notes for Home Your child reviewed subtracting tens, multiple-step problems, and adding and subtracting large numbers. *Home Activity:* Ask your child to choose a number between 30 and 70, add 10 to the number, subtract 20 from the result and tell you the new number. (The new number will be 10 less than the number your child chose.)

Name ___________________________

Practice 12-1

Explore Solid Figures

Use solid figures. Find how many faces, corners, and edges.

	Solid	Name	Faces	Corners	Edges
1.					
2.					
3.					
4.					
5.					

Problem Solving Critical Thinking

What is the same about these solids?

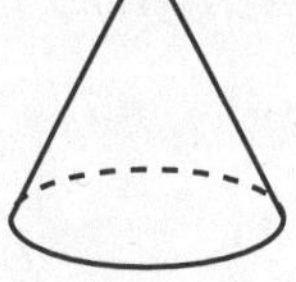

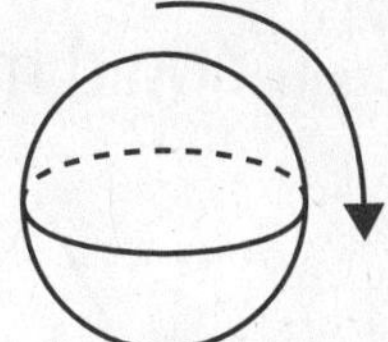

What can they do? ___________________

Draw another shape that belongs.

Notes for Home Your child explored the properties of solid figures. *Home Activity:* Ask your child to look through your kitchen cabinets to find containers that roll and containers that stack.

Name ____________________

Practice 12-2

Explore Solid and Plane Figures

Circle a shape you would make if you traced the face the object is sitting on.

1.    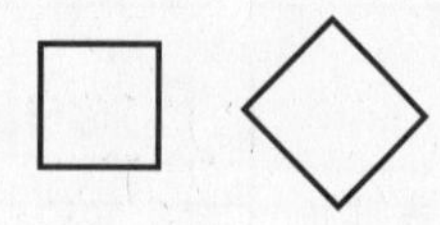

2.   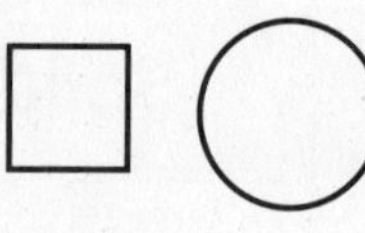

3. 

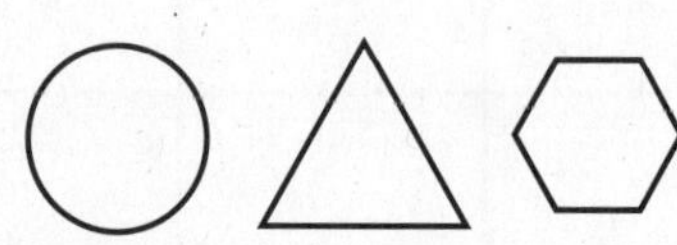

4.    

Problem Solving Visual Thinking

5. Write the name of the solid shape you could make with the pieces.

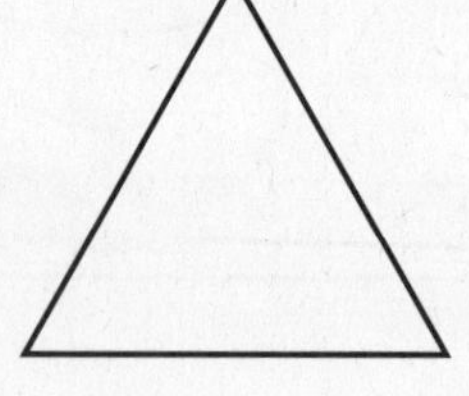 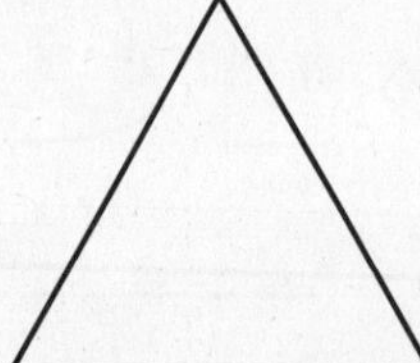

 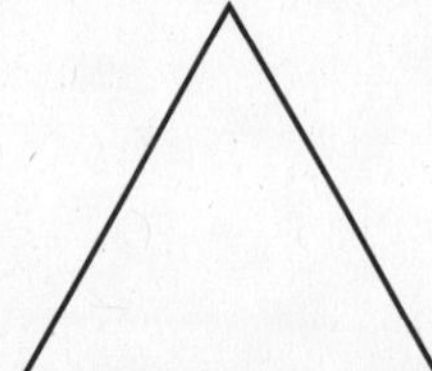

____

Notes for Home Your child explored tracing the faces of solid shapes to make plane figures. *Home Activity:* Ask your child to trace some different shapes from a cereal or cracker box.

Name ______________________________

Practice 12-3

Make Shapes

Write your own. Use pattern blocks.

Make new shapes.

Complete the chart.

	Blocks I Used	New Shape I Made	How many sides?	How many corners?
1.				
2.				

Problem Solving Patterns

3. Draw what comes next.

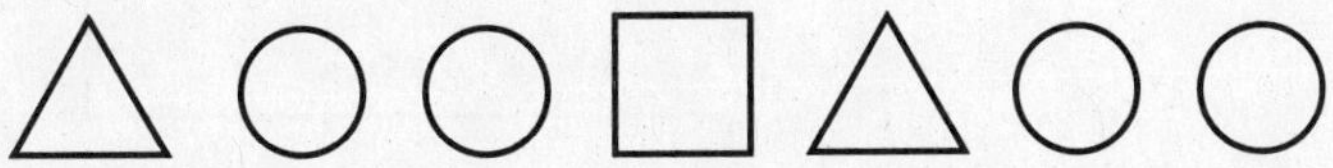

△ ○ ○ □ △ ○ ○

Notes for Home Your child used pattern blocks to make new shapes and found the number of sides and corners for the new shape. *Home Activity:* Using objects such as napkins or paper, ask your child to match the edges to make a new shape and to count the number of sides and corners.

Name ___________________________

Practice 12-4

Congruent Shapes

Draw a shape that is congruent.

1. 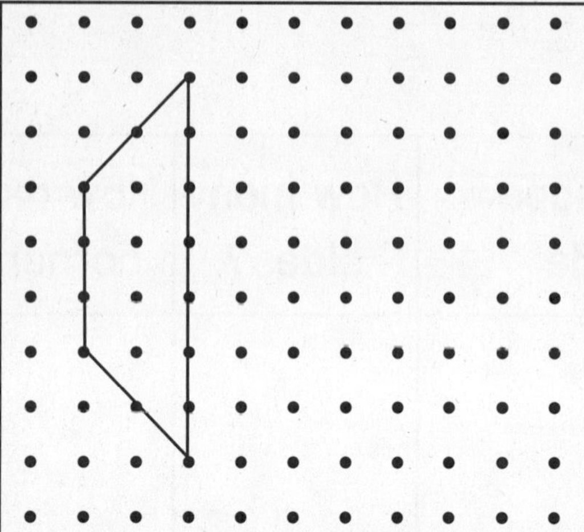

2. 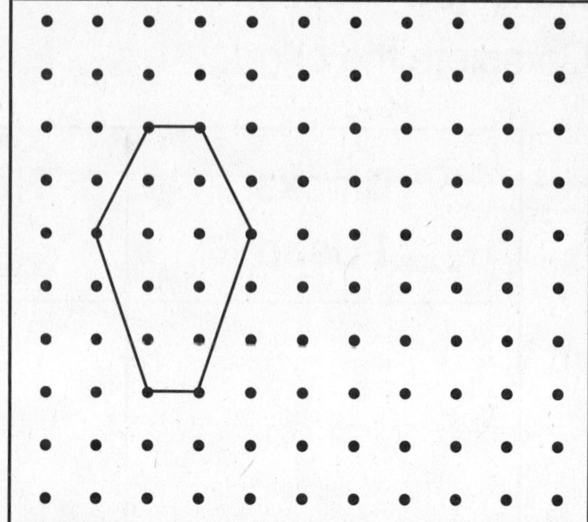

Write your own. Draw a shape. Then have a friend draw a shape that is congruent to your shape..

3. 

4. 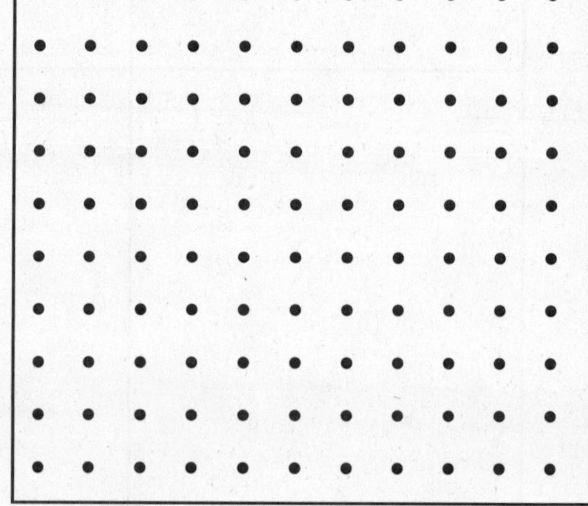

Problem Solving Visual Thinking

5. Draw a shape so there are 5 dots inside and 8 dots on the lines.

Notes for Home Your child practiced drawing figures that are the same size and the same shape. *Home Activity:* Ask your child to look in bureau drawers and on kitchen shelves to find sets of objects that are congruent.

Name ______________________________

Practice 12-5

Slides, Flips, and Turns

Write **slide, flip** or **turn.** Use pattern blocks to check.

1. ______________

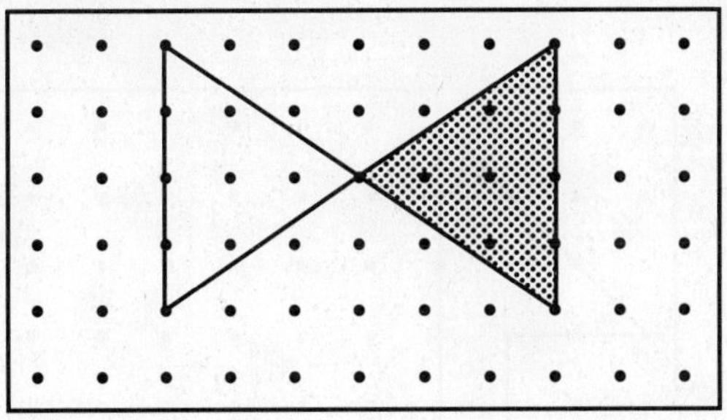

2. ______________

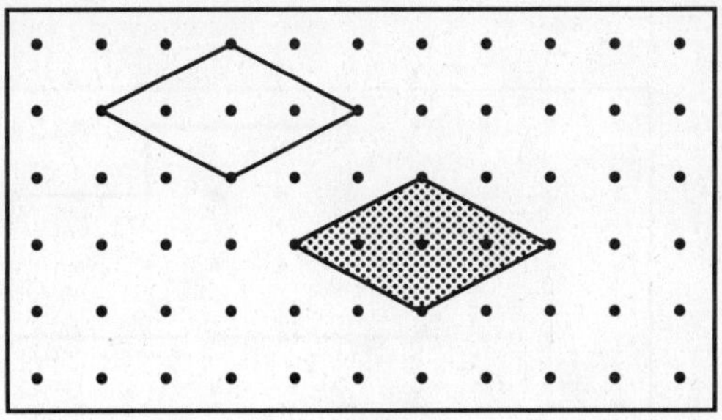

3. ______________

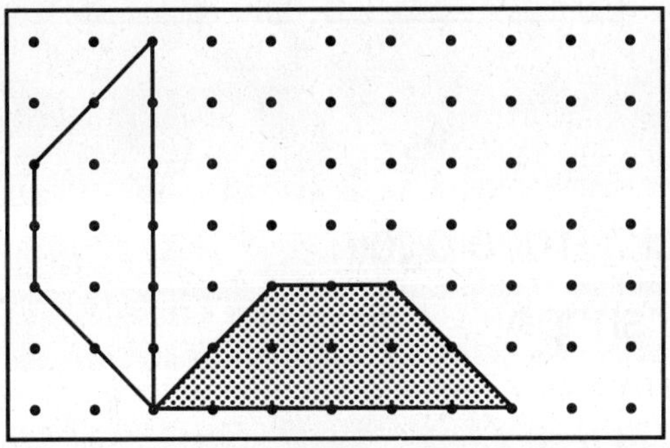

4. ______________

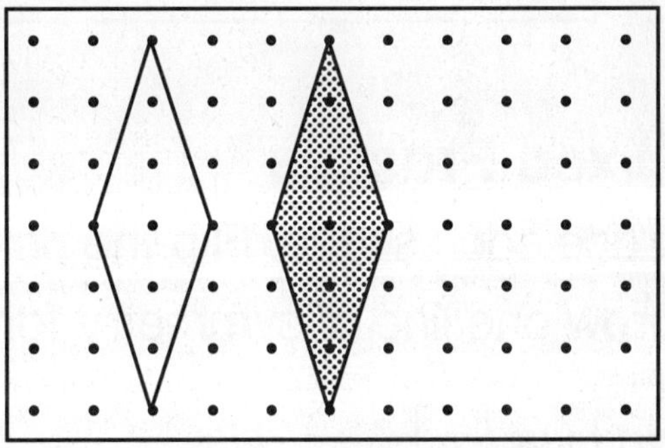

Problem Solving

5. How many of each shape do you need to make a hexagon? Use pattern blocks to help you.

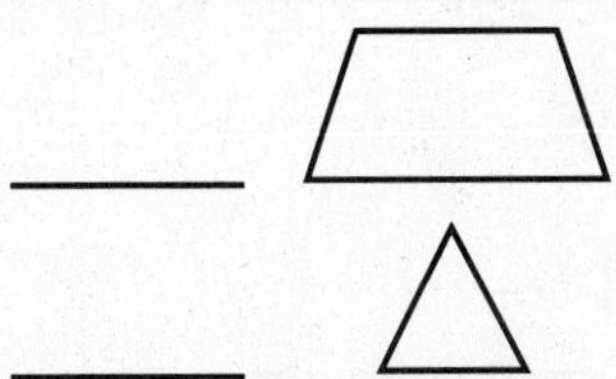

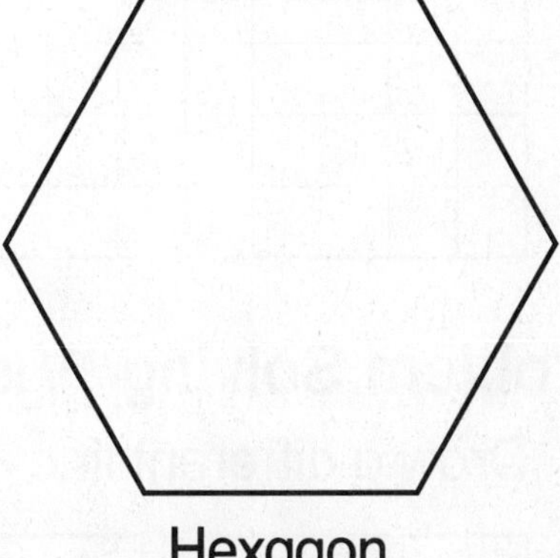

Notes for Home Your child used pattern blocks to tell whether a shape changed by sliding, flipping, or turning. *Home Activity:* Ask your child to use an irregular shape, such as a puzzle piece or spoon, and demonstrate three ways of moving it.

Name ______________________________

Practice 12-6

Symmetry

Make the shapes show symmetry.
Draw to show the matching part.

1. 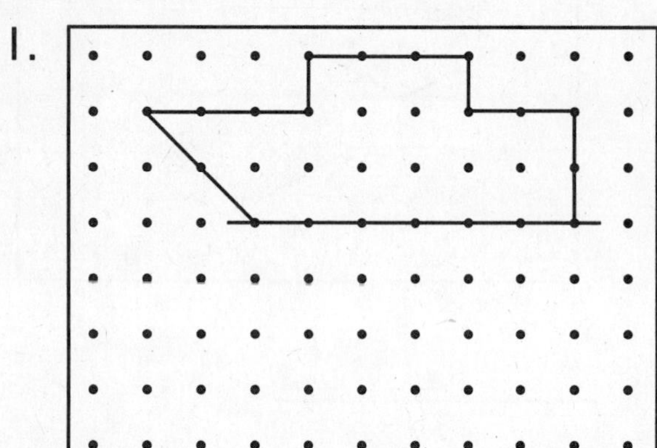

2.

Mixed Practice

Trace each shape. Flip the pattern block. Trace again.
Draw one line of symmetry for the new shape.

3. Use □.

4. Use ◇.

Problem Solving Visual Thinking

5. Draw a different line of symmetry on each shape.

Notes for Home Your child completed shapes to show matching parts and drew lines of symmetry. *Home Activity:* Ask your child to draw one picture that has symmetry and another picture that has no line of symmetry.

Name ______________________________

Practice 12-7

Problem Solving: Use Logical Reasoning

Solve the riddles. Cross out pictures that don't match the clues. Circle the answers.

1. Which plate am I?
   I have a congruent partner.
   I have no stripes.

2. Which sticker am I?
   If you traced around a cube, you would draw my shape.
   I am greater than 3.

3. Which paper hat am I?
   My shape shows symmetry.
   I have more than 3 corners.

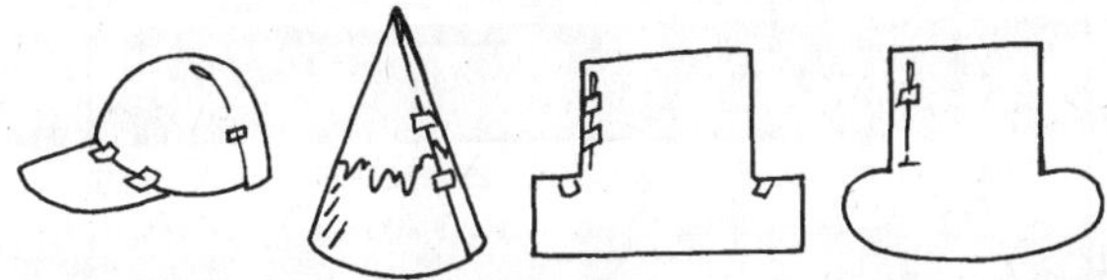

Write About It

4. Write your own riddle.

____

____

____

____

____

Draw your shapes.

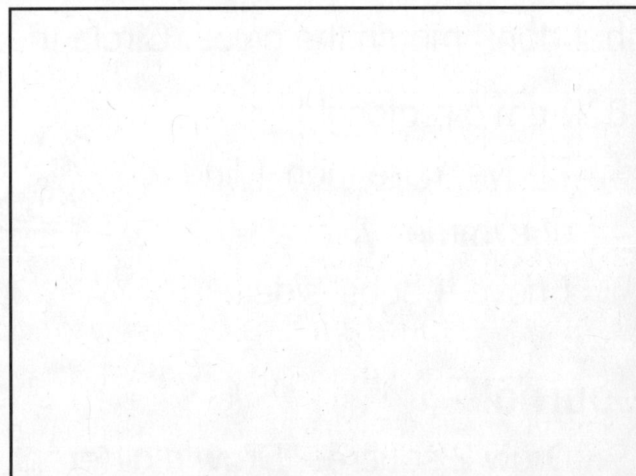

Notes for Home Your child practiced using logical reasoning to solve and make riddles. *Home Activity:* Ask your child to solve this riddle: "I have sides. I have 4 corners. What shape am I—a circle, a triangle, or a square?" (a square)

Name ______________________________

Practice
Chapter 12
A

Mixed Practice: Lessons 1–7

Write how many faces, corners, and edges for this solid.

1. ______ faces 2. ______ corners 3. ______ edges

4. Draw a shape that is congruent.

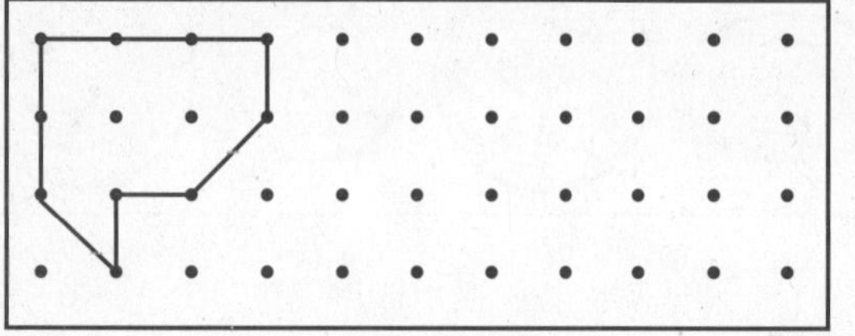

5. Write **slide**, **flip**, or **turn**.

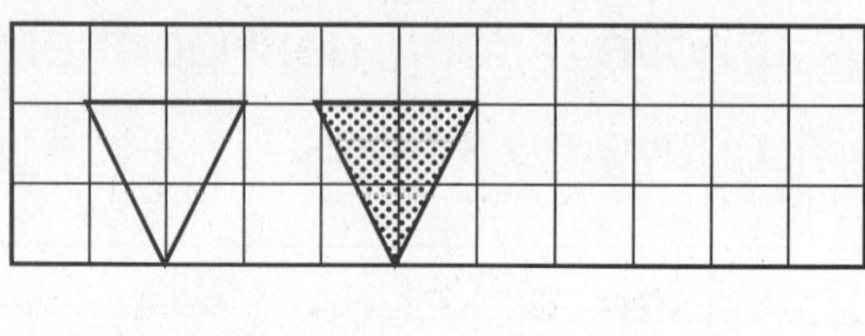

____

Make the shapes show symmetry. Draw matching parts.

6.

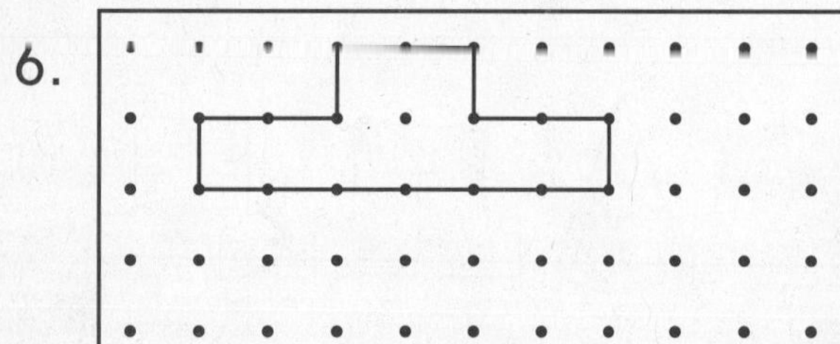

7.

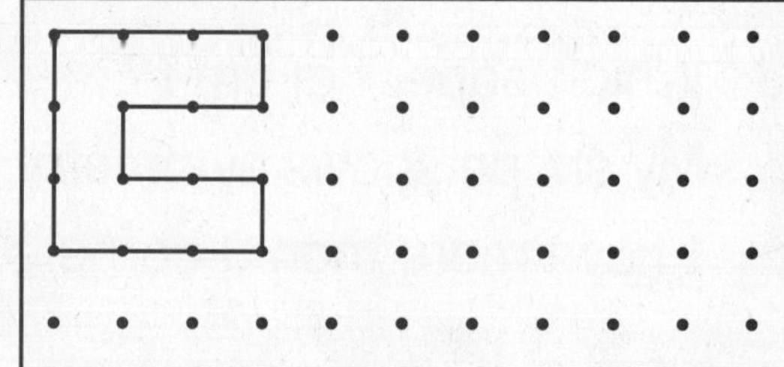

Problem Solving

Solve the riddle. As you read the riddle, cross out the pictures that don't match the clues. Circle the answer.

8. I am a rectangle.
I have more than 1 line of symmetry.
I have 4 equal sides.

Journal

9. Draw 2 squares. Draw a different line of symmetry on each square.

Notes for Home Your child practiced identifying and drawing shapes. *Home Activity:* Play "I Spy" with your child. Look for examples of circles, squares, rectangles, and triangles, and include clues about the number of sides and corners each shape has.

Name ______________________

Practice
Chapters 1–12
A

Cumulative Review

Write the number.

1. forty-eight ______ 2. ninety ______ 3. eighty-one ______

Find the nearest ten. Estimate the sum.

4. 22 + 57

Think:

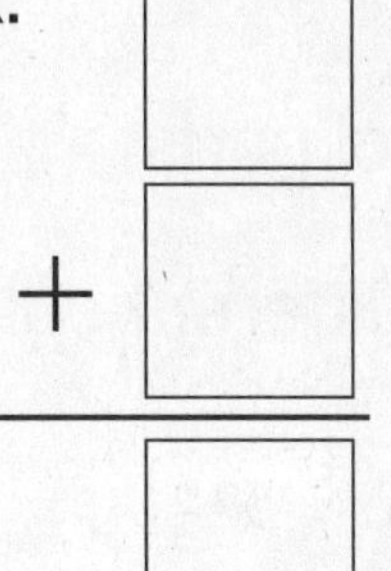

22 + 57 is about ____

5. 38 + 19

Think:

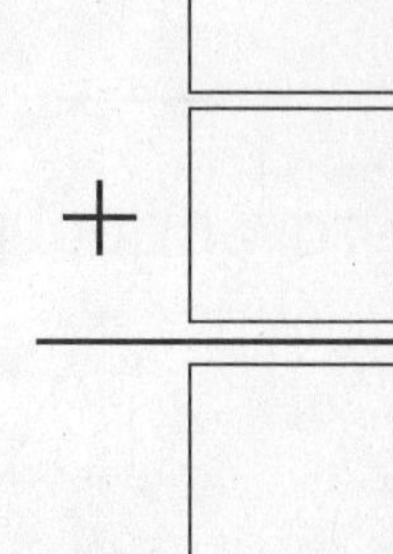

38 + 19 is about ____

Problem Solving

Solve.

6. Jack poured 14 glasses of juice and 27 glasses of lemonade. How many glasses did he pour?

______ glasses

7. Lemonade costs 35¢. A sandwich costs 48¢. How much would you pay for for lemonade and a sandwich?

______ ¢

Test Prep

Fill in the ○ for the correct answer.

8. Find the length in inches.

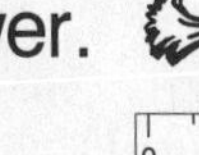

0 1 2 3 4 5 6

○ about 8 inches
○ about 3 inches
○ about 5 inches
○ about 6 inches

Notes for Home Your child reviewed reading and writing numbers, estimating sums, solving problems, and estimating lengths. *Home Activity:* Ask your child to estimate the sum of 19 + 32. (About 50)

Name ______________________________

Practice 12-8

Equal and Unequal Parts

How many equal parts in each shape?

1. 

_____ equal parts _____ equal parts _____ equal parts

Draw equal parts. Color each part a different color.

2.  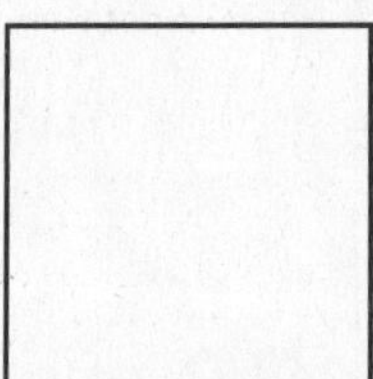 

2 equal parts 4 equal parts 3 equal parts

3. 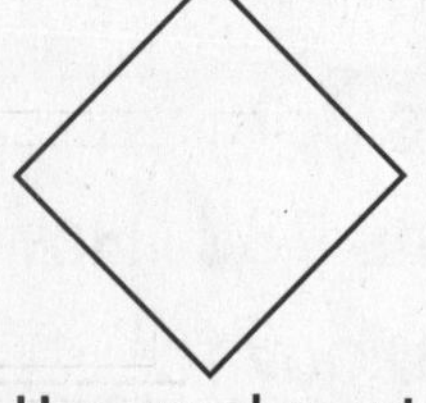  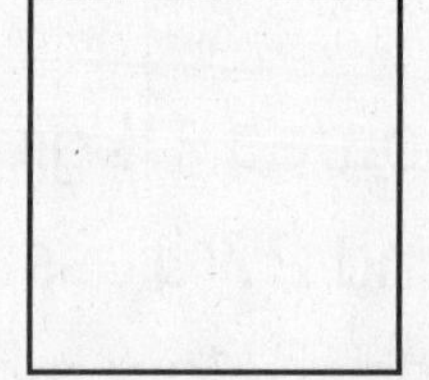

4 equal parts 3 equal parts 6 equal parts

Problem Solving Visual Thinking

Use pattern blocks to make this shape.
Make the shape the same size.
Trace to show the blocks you used.

How many equal parts did you make? _____

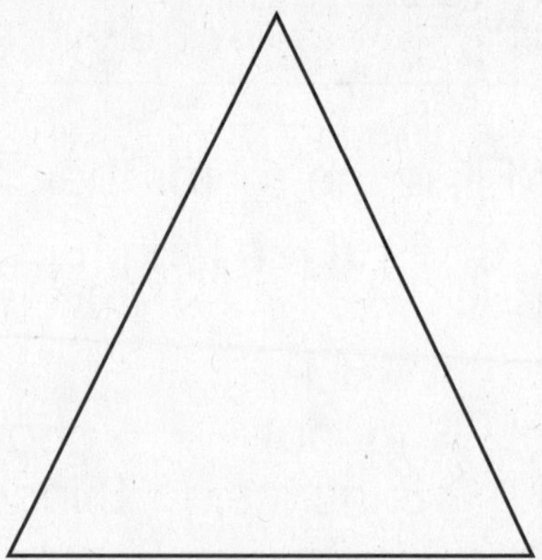

Notes for Home Your child practiced identifying and drawing equal parts. *Home Activity:* Ask your child to show how he or she would divide a food item, such as a pizza, loaf of bread, or stalk of celery, into four equal parts.

Name ______________________________

Practice 12-9

Unit Fractions

Write the fraction for the shaded part.

1.  $\frac{1}{8}$ — 1 part shaded, 8 equal parts in all

2.

3.

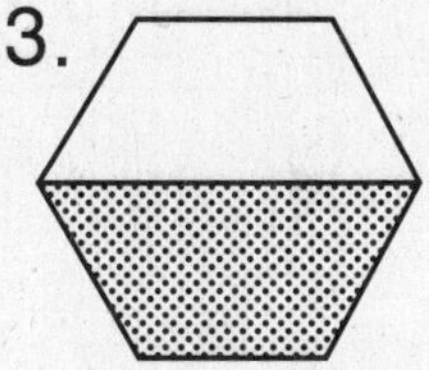

4.

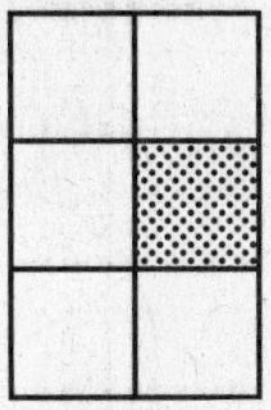

5.

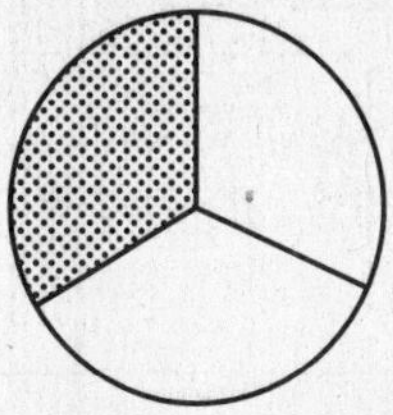

6.

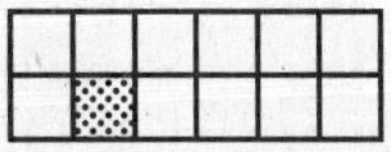

7.

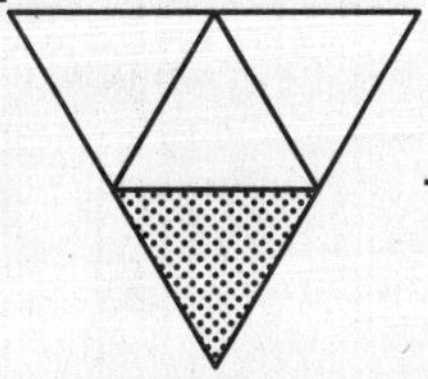

8.

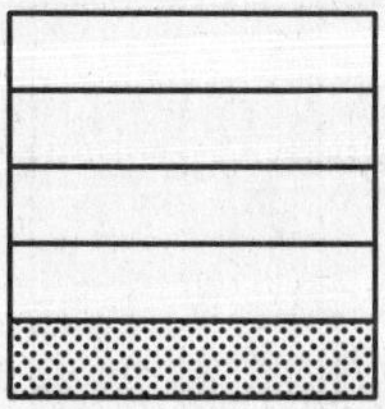

9.

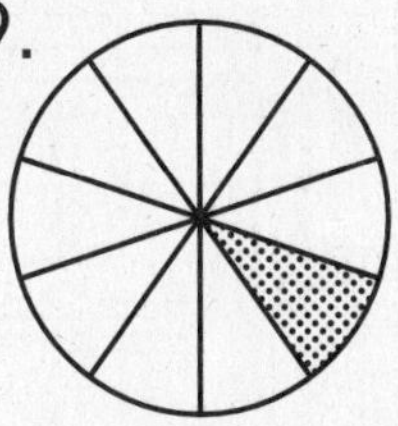

10.

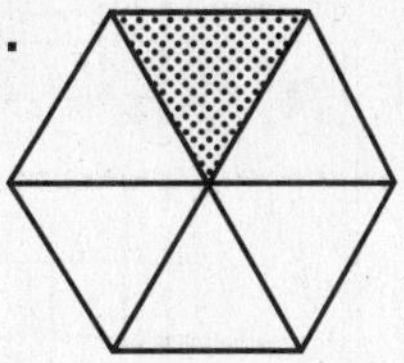

11.

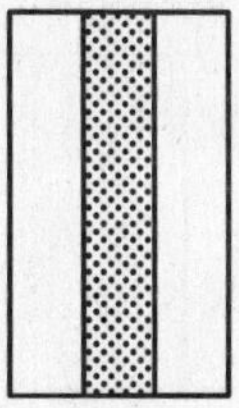

Problem Solving Critical Thinking

12. Is $\frac{1}{3}$ of Jim's fruit pie the same size as $\frac{1}{3}$ of Gina's pie? Why or why not?

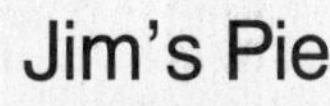

Jim's Pie

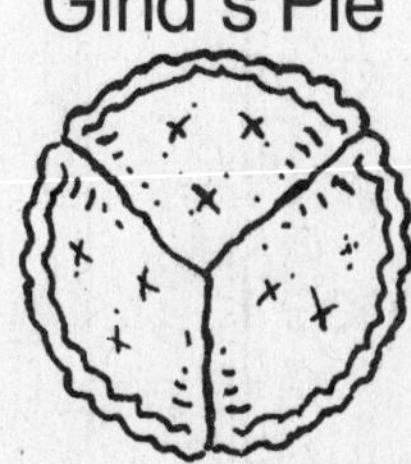

Gina's Pie

____

Notes for Home Your child practiced writing different fractions. *Home Activity:* Draw a circle and ask your child how he or she would draw a line to cut the "pie" into fair shares for 4 people. (Draw two lines to divide the pie into fourths.)

Name ____________________________

Fractions

Practice 12-10

Shade some of the equal parts.

Write the fraction for parts that are shaded.

1. Shade 2 parts.

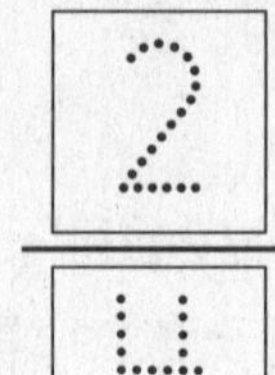

2. Shade 1 part.

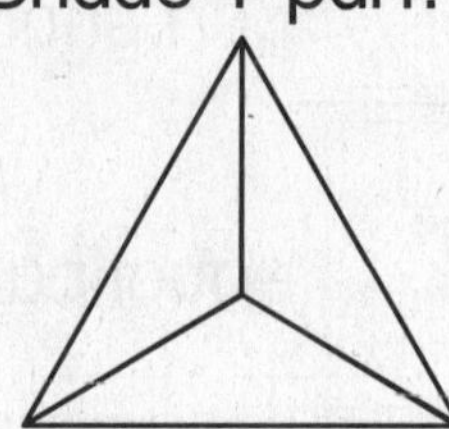

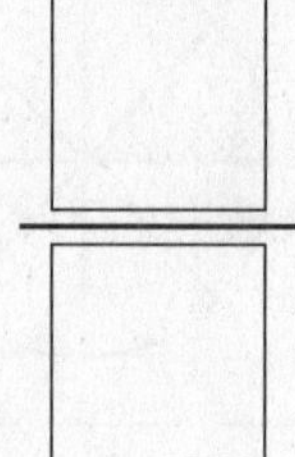

3. Shade 5 parts.

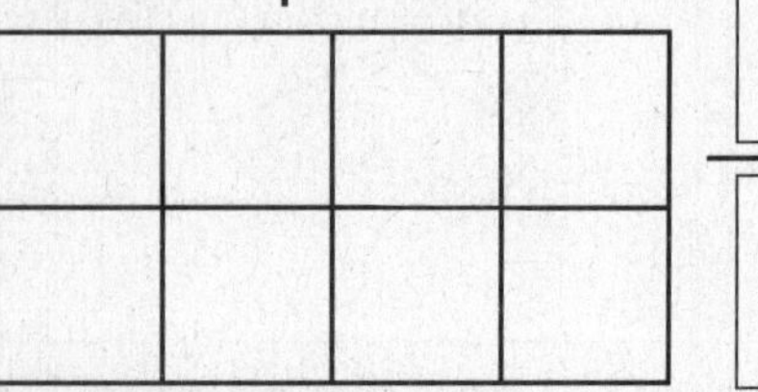

4. Shade 3 parts.

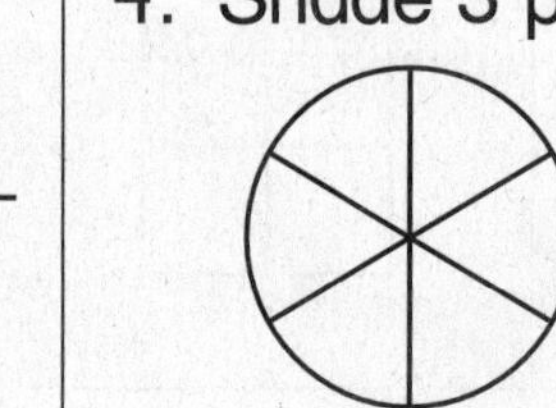

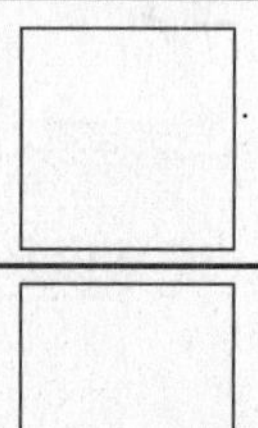

5. Shade 4 parts.

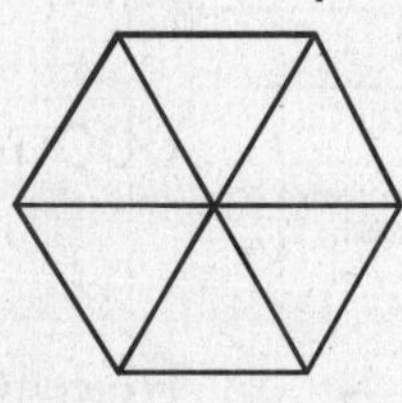

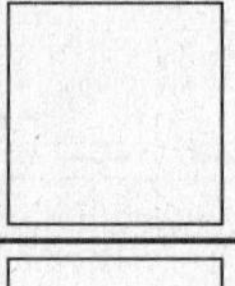

6. Shade 2 parts.

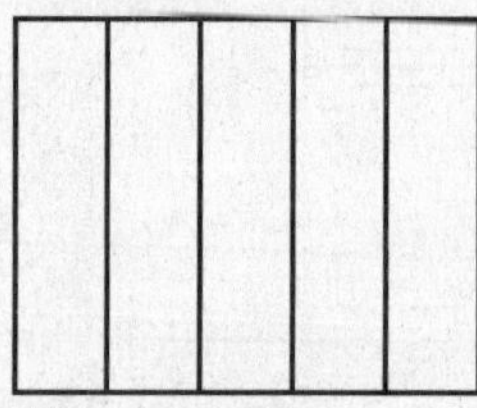

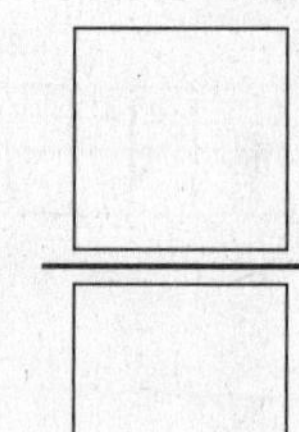

7. Shade 1 part.

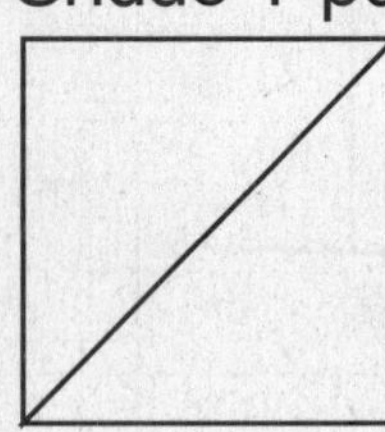

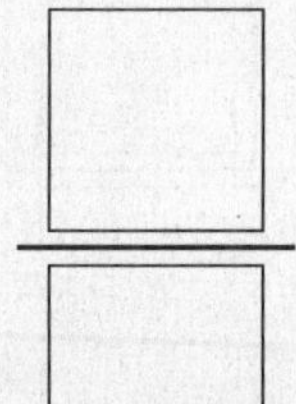

8. Shade 8 parts.

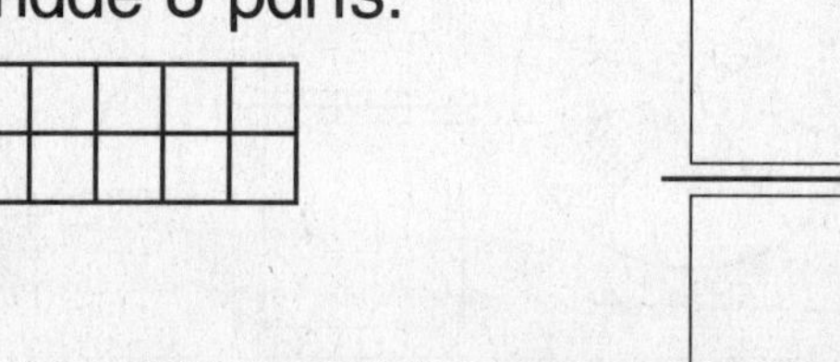

Problem Solving

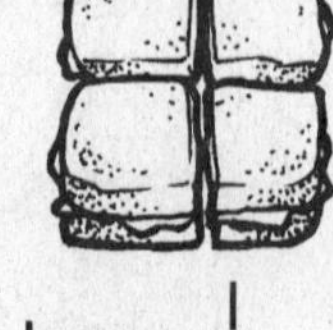

9. Solve.

You ate $\frac{2}{4}$ of a sandwich. Do you have $\frac{1}{2}$ a sandwich left? ______

Write your own problem about a fraction of a sandwich. Have a friend solve it.

____

____

Notes for Home Your child practiced writing fractions. *Home Activity:* Ask you child to shade 2 more parts in exercise 6 and name the fraction. (4/5 — four fifths)

Name ______________________________

Practice 12-11

Estimate Parts of a Whole

How much is **left**? Circle the best estimate.

1.

glass of milk

about $\frac{3}{4}$

about $\frac{1}{8}$

about $\frac{1}{3}$

2.

pita bread

about $\frac{2}{3}$

about $\frac{1}{2}$

about $\frac{5}{6}$

How much **was eaten**? Circle the best estimate.

3.

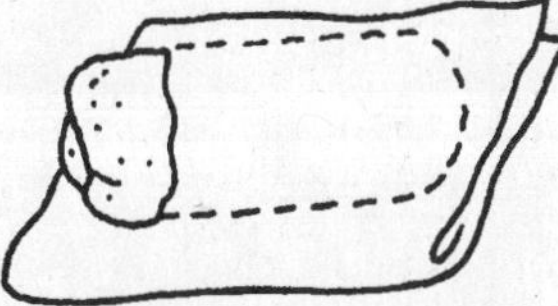

spring roll

about $\frac{1}{2}$

about $\frac{7}{8}$

about $\frac{3}{4}$

4.

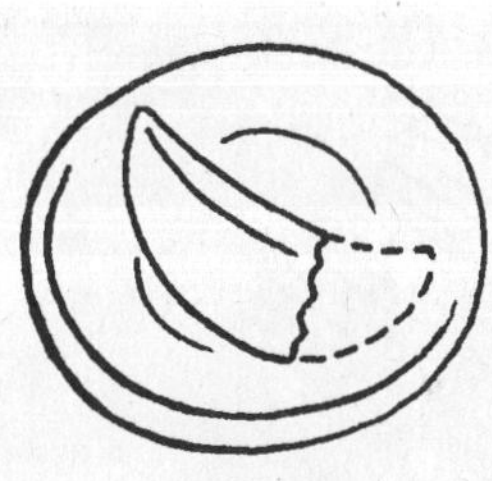

papaya

about $\frac{9}{10}$

about $\frac{1}{3}$

about $\frac{1}{4}$

Problem Solving Visual Thinking

5. Ana filled two glasses from the pitcher. About how many more glasses can she fill?

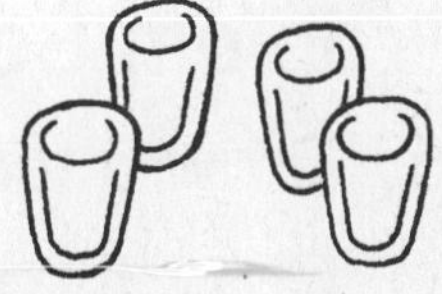

about ______ glasses

Notes for Home Your child used pictures to estimate fractions. *Home Activity:* Ask your child to draw half an apple and tell you the part that is left and the part that is missing. (1/2 is left, 1/2 is missing.)

Name ______________________________

Practice 12-12

Explore a Fraction of a Set

What fraction of each group is striped?

Write the fraction.

1.

_____ striped blocks

_____ blocks in all

are striped.

2.

_____ striped

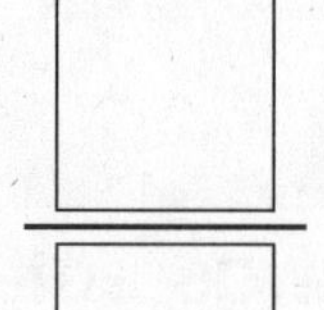

_____ balls in all

are striped.

3.

_____ striped

_____ marbles in all

are striped.

4.

_____ striped

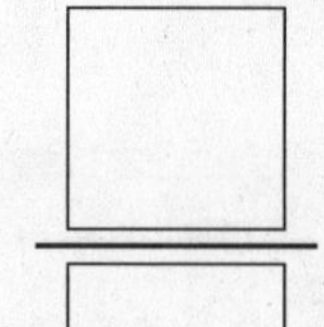

_____ blocks in all

are striped.

Problem Solving

5. Draw 5 tennis balls. Color some green.
   Color the rest yellow.
   What fraction is yellow?

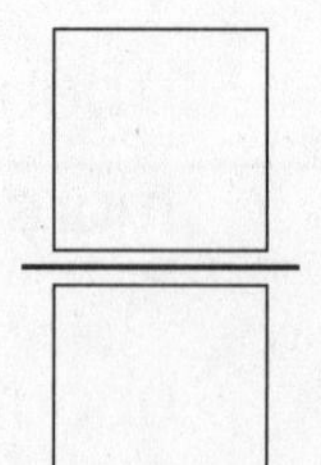

Notes for Home Your child used pictures to write the fraction of a set. *Home Activity:* Display a set of 2 dimes and 4 nickels and ask: "What fraction of the coins are dimes?" (2/6 — two sixths)

Name ______________________________

Fraction of a Set

Practice 12-13

1. Draw a group of buttons.

   Color $\frac{2}{5}$ blue. Color $\frac{3}{5}$ orange.

2. Draw a group of beads.

   Color $\frac{1}{4}$ red. Color $\frac{3}{4}$ black.

3. Draw a group of rings.

   Color $\frac{5}{6}$ green. Color $\frac{1}{6}$ yellow.

Mental Math

Solve.

4. $\frac{1}{4}$ of my bracelets are cotton.
   The rest of my bracelets are plastic.
   What fraction of my bracelets are plastic?

   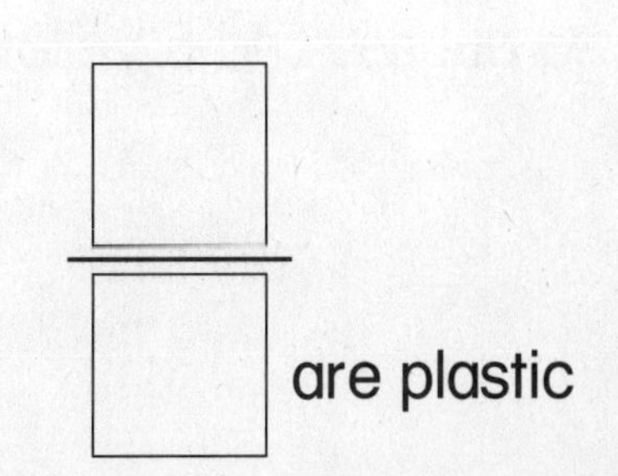

   How many bracelets are plastic? ______

Notes for Home Your child practiced drawing and coloring a group to show a fraction. *Home Activity:* Ask your child to draw and color to show this group: 1/3 of the apples are green. 2/3 of the apples are red. (Draw 1 green and 2 red apples.)

Name ____________________

Practice 12-14

Explore Probability

Reach in the bag and pick 1 cube at a time.
Write what color you pick on a piece of paper.
Put the cube back in the bag. Pick 10 times in all.

1. Put red, blue, and yellow cubes in a bag. Make the red cubes more likely to be picked. Use 30 cubes in all.

   Do the activity.

Number of cubes in my bag.	My results.
R ____	R ____
B ____	B ____
Y ____	Y ____

2. Put red, blue, and yellow cubes in a bag. Make the yellow cubes more likely to be picked. Use 30 cubes in all.

   Do the activity.

Number of cubes in my bag.	My results.
R ____	R ____
B ____	B ____
Y ____	Y ____

Journal

3. Why are you more likely to pick blue if you have 10 blue cubes, 5 red cubes, and 5 yellow cubes in a bag? Explain.

Notes for Home Your child made up and completed a probability activity. *Home Activity:* Ask your child to collect a group of 2 different kinds of objects so that one kind of object is more likely to be picked, and then show you how to complete a probability experiment like the one above.

Name ______________________________

Problem Solving: Make a Prediction

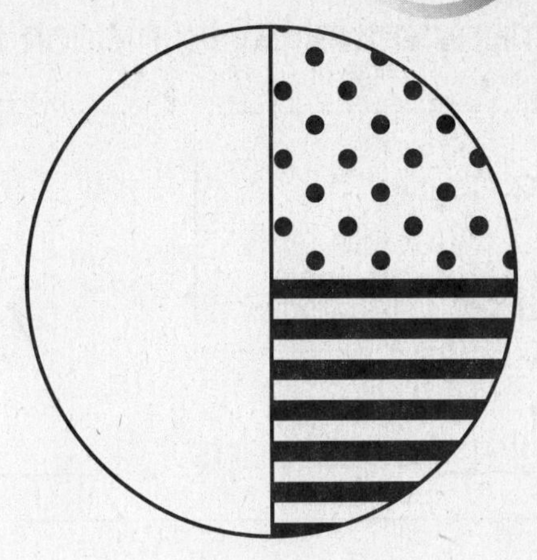

1. Predict. If you were to spin once, would this spinner be more likely to land on plain, dots, or stripes?

   What makes you think so?

   ____

   ____

2. Predict. If you were to spin 12 times, how many times would the spinner land on plain? _____ On dots? _____ On stripes? _____

3. Spin 12 times. Color a square for each spin. Write the results.

_____ plain
_____ dots
_____ stripes

Write About It

Write whether the outcome is certain, cannot happen or is likely to happen.

4. land on stripes ______________________________

5. land on plain ______________________________

6. land on dots ______________________________

Notes for Home Your child practiced making predictions. *Home Activity:* Ask your child to predict what time the sun will go down tonight.

Name ________________________________

Mixed Practice: Lessons 8–15

How many equal parts in each shape?

1. 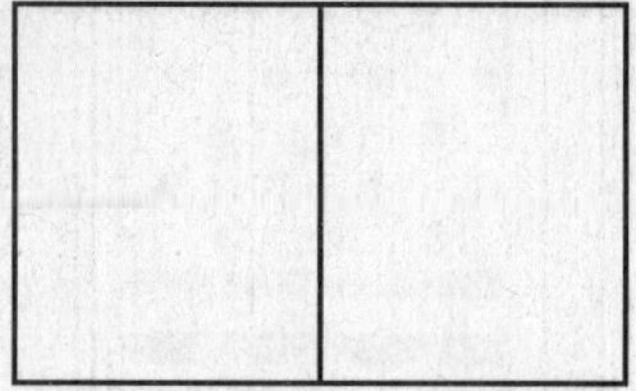 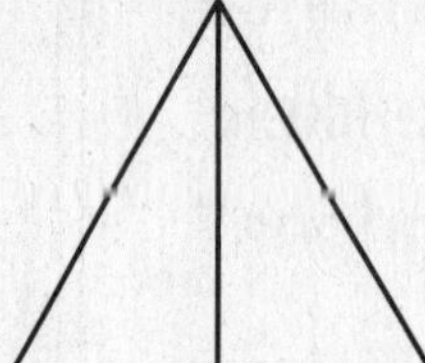 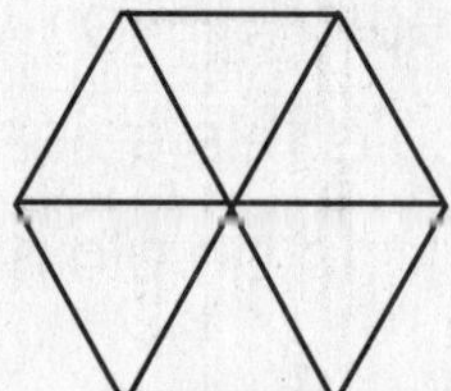

_____ equal parts _____ equal parts _____ equal parts

Write the fraction for the shaded part.

2. 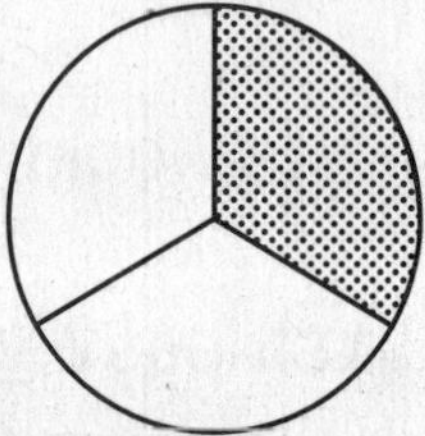

3. 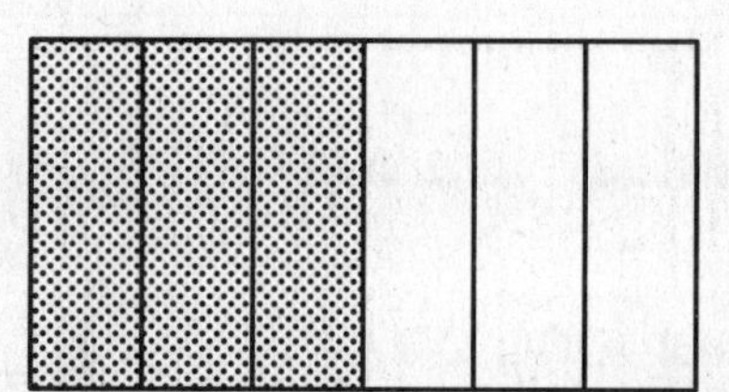

How much is left?
Circle the best estimate.

4. 

about $\frac{1}{3}$

about $\frac{1}{2}$

Draw a group of marbles.
Color $\frac{3}{5}$ yellow. Color $\frac{2}{5}$ blue.

5. 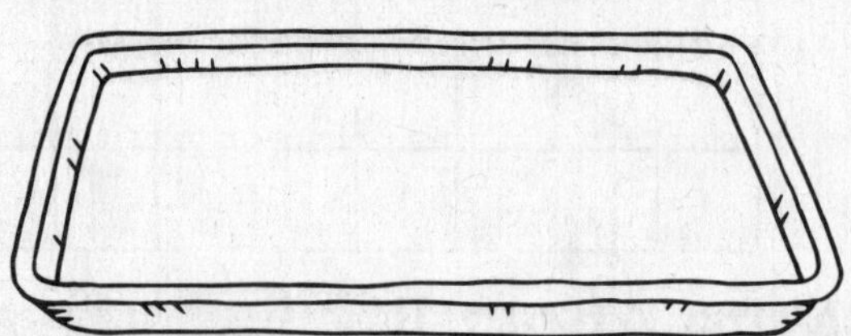

Problem Solving

6. Predict. If you were to spin this spinner once, would it be more likely to land on plain, dots, or stripes? ______________

Journal

7. How does knowing about equal parts help you if you want to share a pizza with friends? Explain.

Notes for Home Your child practiced identifying fractions. *Home Activity:* Ask your child to show you a way to cut a sandwich or piece of toast into 4 equal parts.

Name ______________________________

Practice
Chapters 1–12
B

Cumulative Review

Add or subtract.

1.

38	65	57	60	42	83
− 9	− 24	− 13	+ 20	− 8	− 45

2.

29	74	31	50	76	47
+ 46	− 20	− 18	+ 17	− 26	− 19

Problem Solving

3. Jason made 15 jelly sandwiches. He made 23 tuna sandwiches. How many sandwiches did he make in all?

_____ sandwiches

4. Mee has 45 oranges to sell. She sells 26 oranges to Jason's class. How many does she have left to sell?

_____ oranges

Test Prep

Fill in the ○ for the correct answer.

5. Choose the correct symbol to compare the numbers.

45 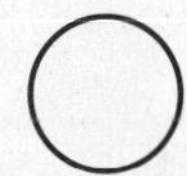 36

○ <  = ○ >

6. Which numbers are in order from greatest to least?

○ 7, 42, 103, 324, 15

○ 324, 103, 42, 15, 7

○ 7, 15, 42, 103, 324

Notes for Home Your child reviewed adding and subtracting two-digit numbers, comparing numbers, and ordering numbers. *Home Activity:* Ask your child to subtract 37–18. (19)

Name ______________________

Practice 13-1

Explore Joining Equal Groups

You can add to find how many oranges in all.

4 + 4 + 4 + 4 = 16

Use counters to show the oranges.
Find how many oranges in all.

		Draw the oranges.	How many oranges in all?
1.	1 bag		4
2.	2 bags		4 + 4 = ____
3.	3 bags		4 + 4 + 4 = ____
4.	4 bags		4 + 4 + 4 + 4 = ____

Talk About It How could you find out how many oranges would be in 5 bags?

____

Notes for Home Your child made equal groups and added to find how many in all. *Home Activity:* Ask your child to use objects such as spoons to make 4 groups of 3 objects each. Ask your child to add to find how many objects in all. (12)

 Use with pages 493–494.

Name ______________________________

Addition and Multiplication

Find how many in all. You can use cubes.

1. How many wheels?
   3 groups of 3

___ + ___ + ___ = ___

___ × ___ = ___

2. How many sails?
   3 groups of 2

___ + ___ + ___ = ___

___ × ___ = ___

3. How many tennis balls?
   4 groups of 3

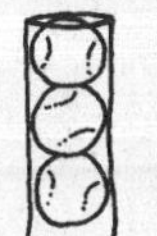
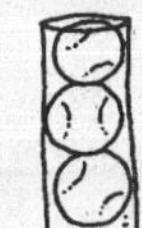

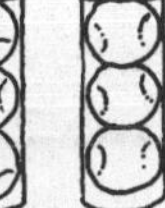

___ + ___ + ___ + ___ = ___

___ × ___ = ___

4. How many marbles?
   3 groups of 6

___ + ___ + ___ = ___

___ × ___ = ___

Problem Solving Visual Thinking

Can you multiply to tell how many in all?
Tell why or why not.

5. 
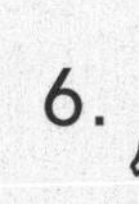

yes no

6. 

yes no

7. 

yes no

Notes for Home Your child added and multiplied to find the total number in several groups. *Home Activity:* Ask your child to find the total number of wheels for 5 bicycles with 2 wheels each. (5 x 2 = 10)

Name ______________________

Practice 13-3

Explore Building Arrays

2 rows of 6 bowling pins

$2 \times 6 = 12$

There are 12 bowling pins in all.

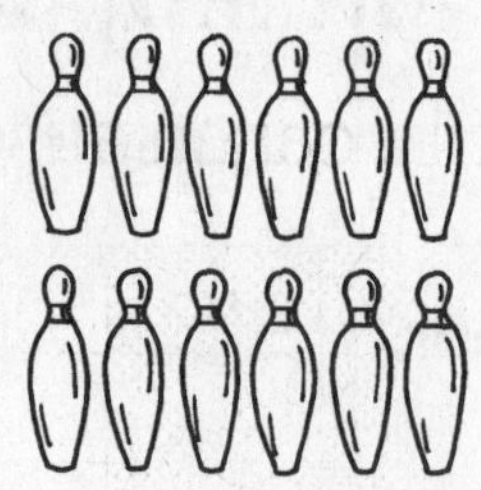

Color equal rows. Write how many. Find the product.

1. Show 5 rows of 3

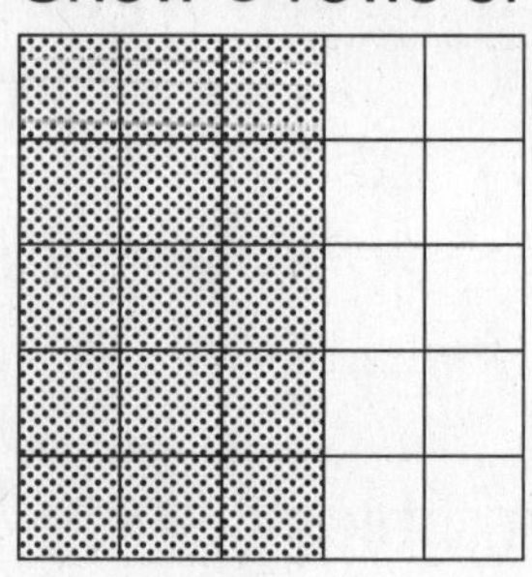

5 rows

3 in each row

$5 \times 3 = 15$

2. Show 4 rows of 4

_____ rows

_____ in each row

$4 \times 4 =$ ____

3. Show 2 rows of 5

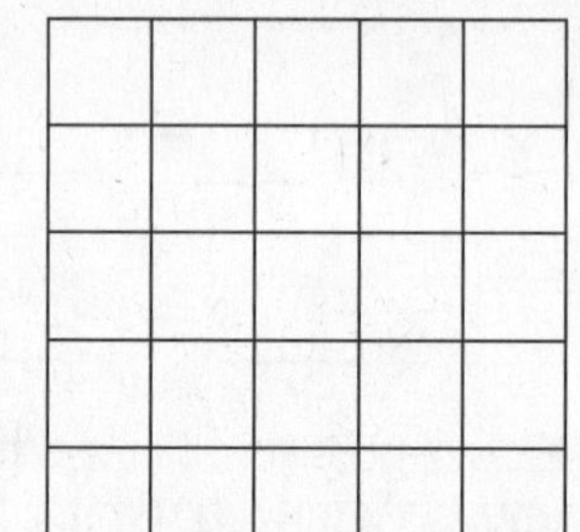

_____ rows

_____ in each row

$2 \times 5 =$ ____

Problem Solving

4. Draw groups to show 3 x 4.

How many in all? _____

5. Draw groups to show 4 x 6.

How many in all? _____

Notes for Home Your child colored equal rows on a grid and completed a multiplication number sentence. *Home Activity:* Draw a picture which shows 3 groups of 7 objects and ask your child to write the multiplication sentence. (3 x 7 = 21)

 Use with pages 497–498.

Name ______________________

Practice 13-4

Multiplication in Any Order

Find the product. You can use cubes.

1. 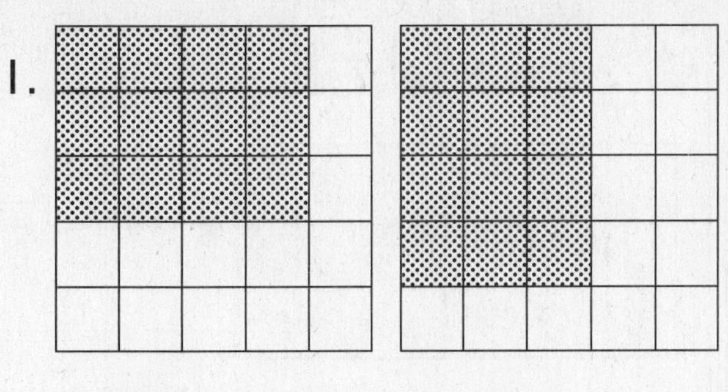

$3 \times 4 =$ ____ $4 \times 3 =$ ____

2. 

$5 \times 2 =$ ____ $2 \times 5 =$ ____

Write your own. Use the same numbers. Color different rows.
Write different multiplication sentences.

3. 

____ $\times$ ____ $=$ ____

4.

____ $\times$ ____ $=$ ____

5. $7 \times 2 =$ ____

$2 \times 7 =$ ____

6. $6 \times 3 =$ ____

$3 \times 6 =$ ____

7. $3 \times 5 =$ ____

$5 \times 3 =$ ____

Problem Solving Patterns

8. Find the products. What pattern do you see?

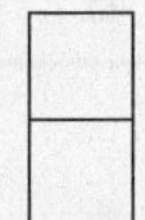

$2 \times 1 =$ ____

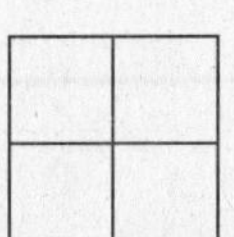

$2 \times 2 =$ ____

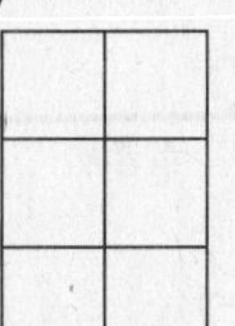

$2 \times 3 =$ ____

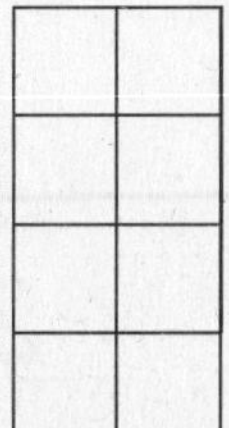

$2 \times 4 =$ ____

Notes for Home Your child found answers to related multiplication facts. *Home Activity:* Ask your child to arrange rows of pennies to show related multiplication facts such as 3 x 2 and 2 x 3.

Name ______________________________

Practice 13-5

Multiplication in Vertical Form

Write the multiplication fact in two ways.

1. 3 rows of 6

3 × 6 = 18

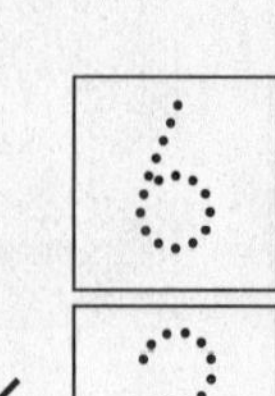

$$\begin{array}{r} 6 \\ \times\ 3 \\ \hline 18 \end{array}$$

2. 2 groups of 7

____ × ____ = ____

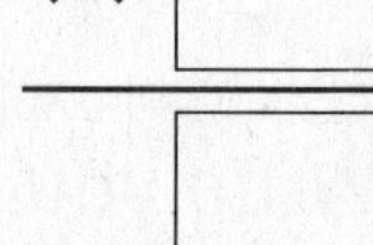

3. 4 rows of 3

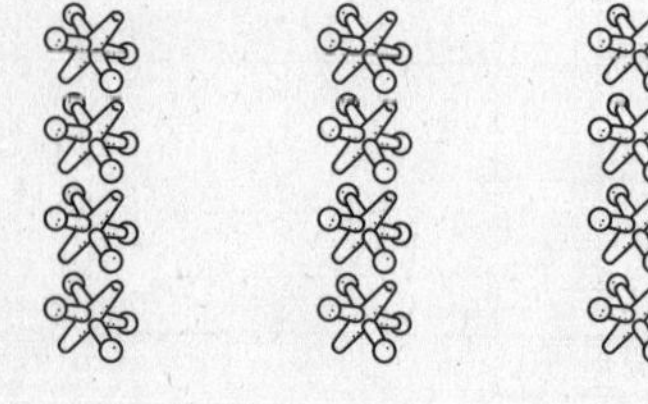

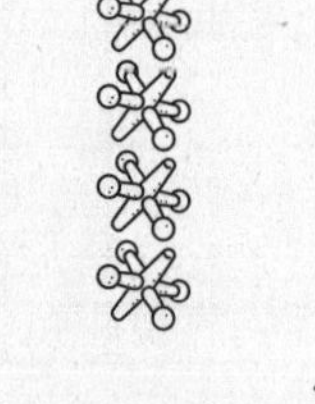

____ × ____ = ____

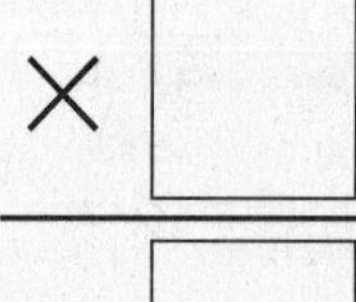

4. 5 rows of 4

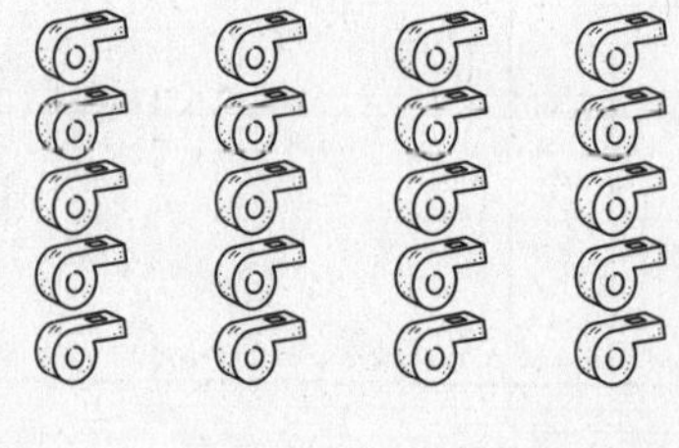

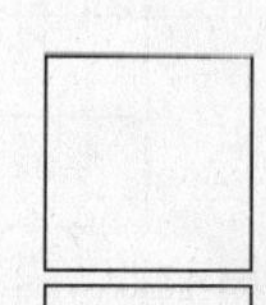

____ × ____ = ____

Problem Solving Patterns

5. Find the number pattern. Write the missing numbers.

$$\begin{array}{r} 2 \\ \times 1 \\ \hline \end{array} \quad \begin{array}{r} 2 \\ \times 2 \\ \hline \end{array} \quad \begin{array}{r} 2 \\ \times 3 \\ \hline \end{array} \quad \begin{array}{r} 2 \\ \times \square \\ \hline \end{array} \quad \begin{array}{r} 2 \\ \times \square \\ \hline \end{array} \quad \begin{array}{r} 2 \\ \times \square \\ \hline \end{array}$$

Notes for Home Your child wrote multiplication facts in two different ways. *Home Activity:* Have your child write the multiplication fact for 3 groups of 4 two different ways.

Name ______________________________

Problem Solving: Choose a Strategy

Practice 13-6

Choose a way to solve each problem.
Show what you did.

1. Jamal packed 5 bananas in each of 4 bags. How many bananas did he pack?

2. Kendra and Miguel each packed 8 baskets with fruit. How many baskets did they pack in all?

3. Erin made 6 gift baskets. Julie made 6 gift baskets. Andy made 6 gift baskets. How many gift baskets did the children make in all?

Problem Solving Estimation

4. About how many mangos are ready to be packed?

   Circle the best estimate.

about 20 about 40 about 60

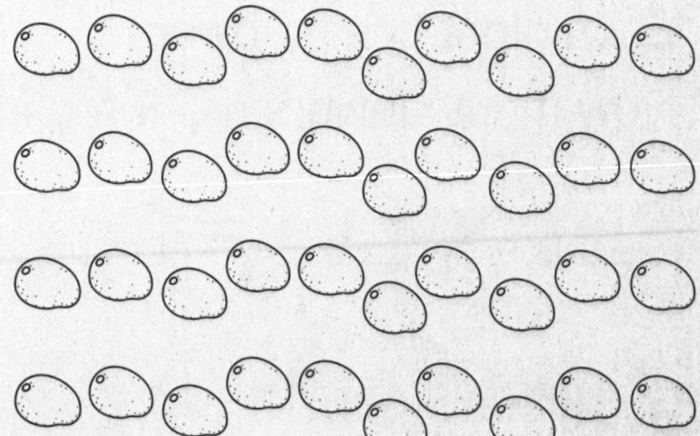

Notes for Home Your child chose strategies to solve problems involving multiplication. *Home Activity:* Ask your child to solve this problem: *6 children packed 2 gift baskets each. How many baskets did they pack?* (6 x 2 = 12)

Name ______________________________

Practice
Chapter 13
A

Mixed Practice: Lessons 1–6

Find how many in all. You can use snap cubes.

1. How many grapes?
   4 groups of 4 grapes

_____ + _____ + _____ + _____ = _____ grapes

_____ × _____ = _____ grapes

Color equal rows. Find the product.

2. 4 rows of 3   3 rows of 4

$4 \times 3 =$ _____ $3 \times 4 =$ _____

3. 5 rows of 2   2 rows of 5

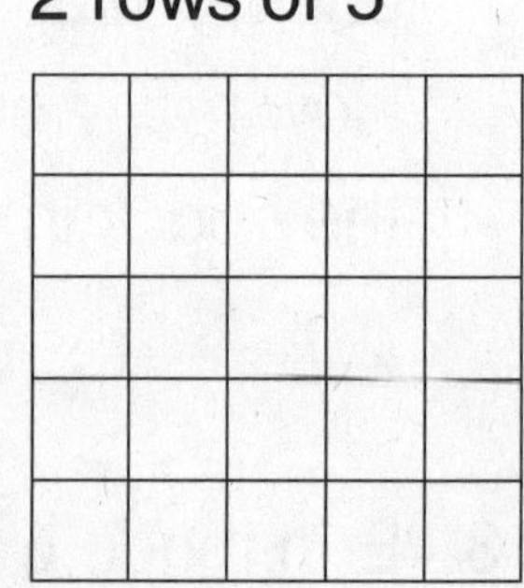

$5 \times 2 =$ _____ $2 \times 5 =$ _____

Problem Solving

Draw a picture to solve the problem.

4. There are 3 plants on a shelf.
   Each plant has 5 flowers.
   How many flowers are there in all?

   _____ × _____ = _____ flowers

Journal

5. Tell two ways you can find the total number of 3 + 3 + 3 + 3.

Notes for Home Your child practiced using pictures and drawing pictures to solve multiplication problems.
Home Activity: Ask your child to explain how he or she responded to the Journal question.

Name ______________________________

Practice
Chapters 1–13
A

Cumulative Review

Shade some of the equal parts.
Write the fraction for the parts that are shaded.

1. Shade 5 equal parts.

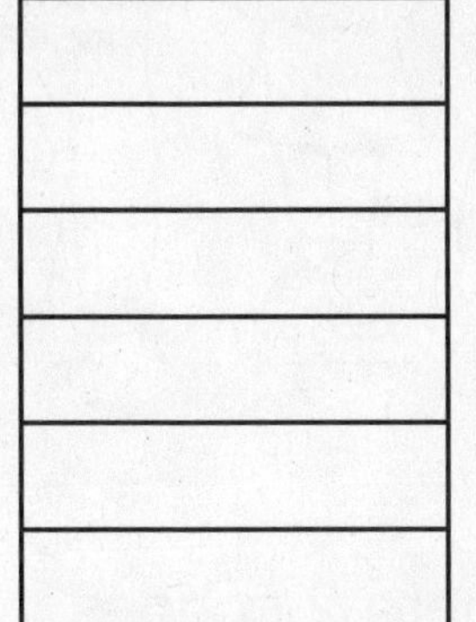

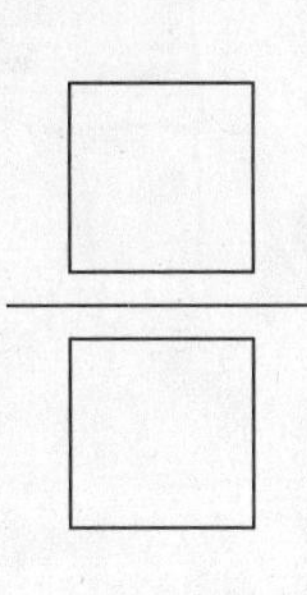

2. Shade 3 equal parts.

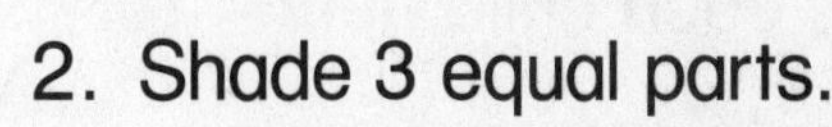

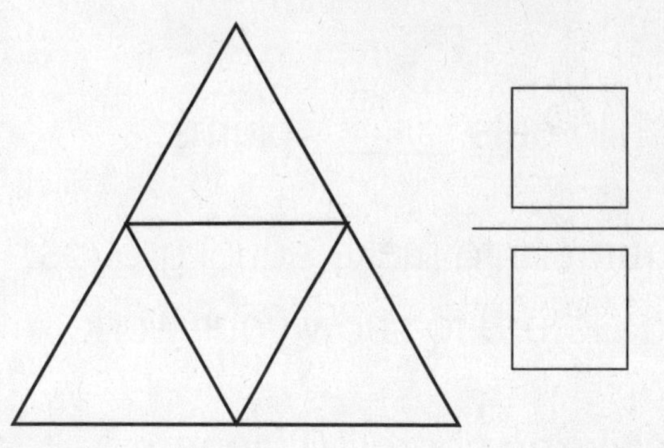

Getting Ready for Next Year

Copy each problem on a separate piece of paper. Add or subtract.

3.

346	493	851	172	685	574
+ 125	− 268	− 419	+ 634	− 372	+ 185

Test Prep

Fill in the ○ for the correct answer.
Which shape would you make if you traced a face of each object?

4.

5.

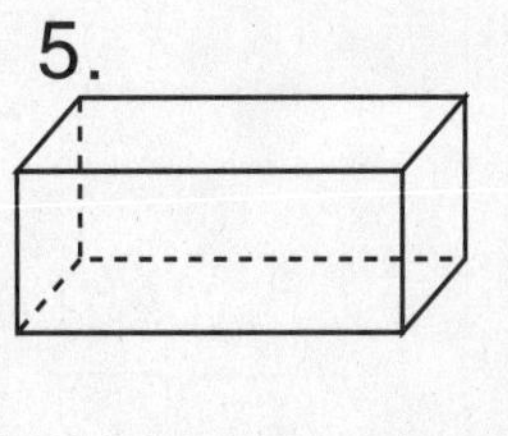

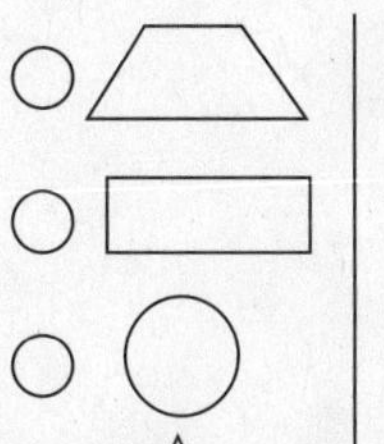

6.

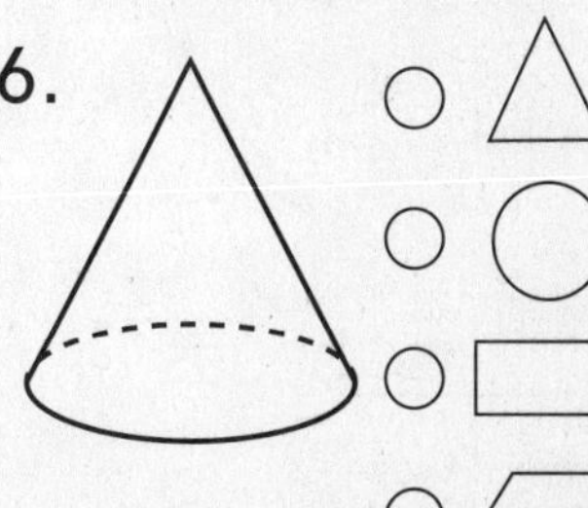

Notes for Home Your child reviewed fractions, solids, and addition and subtraction. *Home Activity:* Provide your child with an unopened can and ask him or her to show you one of the faces that is a circle.

Name ______________________________

Practice 13-7

Explore Making Equal Groups

At camp, 4 children share 12 plums equally. How many plums does each child get?

Each child gets __3__ plums.

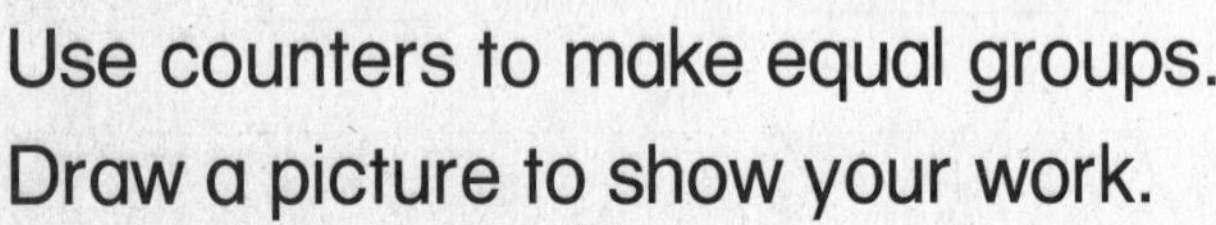

Use counters to make equal groups. Draw a picture to show your work.

1. 5 children share 10 flippers. How many flippers for each child?

   __2__ flippers

2. 6 children share 2 canoes. How many children in each canoe?

   ______ children

3. 3 children share 15 beads. How many beads for each child?

   ______ beads

4. 12 children share 2 tents. How many children in each tent?

   ______ children

Talk About It Could 3 children share 7 ears of corn equally? How do you know?

Notes for Home Your child drew pictures to share amounts equally. *Home Activity:* Give your child 8 pennies or other small objects and ask him or her to show you how to share them equally with you.

Name ______________________________

Practice 13-8

Share and Divide

You can use counters. Draw a picture to show equal groups. Write the number sentence.

1. 12 balls in 3 boxes.

12 ÷ 3 = 4 balls

2. 16 pencils in 2 boxes.

____ ÷ ____ = ____ pencils

3. 18 beads in 3 bags.

____ ÷ ____ = ____ beads

4. 8 oranges in 4 bags.

____ ÷ ____ = ____ oranges

5. 20 peanuts in 5 bags.

____ ÷ ____ = ____ peanuts

6. 6 apples shared by 2 children.

____ ÷ ____ = ____ apples

Problem Solving

Solve. You can use counters.

7. Suli has 12 hula hoops to pass out in the playground. If she gives 2 hula hoops to each child, how many children will get hula hoops?

_____ children

Notes for Home Your child drew pictures and completed number sentences. *Home Activity:* Ask your child to draw a picture and write a division sentence to show 14 hula hoops shared by 7 children. (14 ÷ 7 = 2)

Name ______________________________

Practice 13-9

Problem Solving:
Choose an Operation

Circle the number sentence that helps you solve the problem.

1. 7 children were hiking. Each child found 3 acorns. How many acorns did the children find?

$7 - 3 = 4$ $21 \div 7 = 3$ $7 \times 3 = 21$

2. 15 children take swim class. The coaches separate them into 3 equal groups. How many children are in each group?

$5 \times 3 = 15$ $15 \div 3 = 5$ $15 + 3 = 18$

3. 9 children enter a running race. 6 children finish the race. How many children didn't finish?

$9 \div 3 = 6$ $9 - 6 = 3$ $3 + 6 = 9$

Tell a Math Story

Tell a story for each number sentence.

4. $15 - 5 = 10$ 5. $10 \div 2 = 5$ 6. $8 \times 2 = 16$

Notes for Home Your child identified a number sentence that could be used to solve a word problem.
Home Activity: Ask your child to tell you a word problem for Exercise 5. (Possible answer: 10 children play a game. They play in 2 equal teams. How many children are on each team? 5)

Name ______________________________

Mixed Practice: Lessons 7–9

You can use counters to make equal groups.
Draw a picture to show your work.
Write the number sentence.

1. 9 children share 3 benches equally. How many children at each bench?

____ ÷ ____ = ____ children

2. 14 balls go in 2 boxes equally. How many balls in each box?

____ ÷ ____ = ____ balls

Problem Solving

Circle the number sentence that solves the problem.

3. At a picnic, 4 people share 12 ears of corn equally. How many ears of corn did each person get?

$4 \times 3 = 12$　　$12 \div 4 = 3$　　$12 - 4 = 8$

4. There are 5 children playing with hula hoops. Each child has 2 hula hoops. How many hula hoops are there?

$5 \times 2 = 10$　　$5 + 2 = 7$　　$10 \div 5 = 2$

Journal

5. Write a story for this number sentence. **8 ÷ 4 = 2**

Notes for Home Your child practiced multiplying and dividing. *Home Activity:* Ask your child to draw to find how many balls there are if 5 children each have 3 balls. (5 x 3 = 15)

Name ____________________

Practice
Chapters 1–13
B

Cumulative Review

Draw a shape that is congruent to each shape.

1. 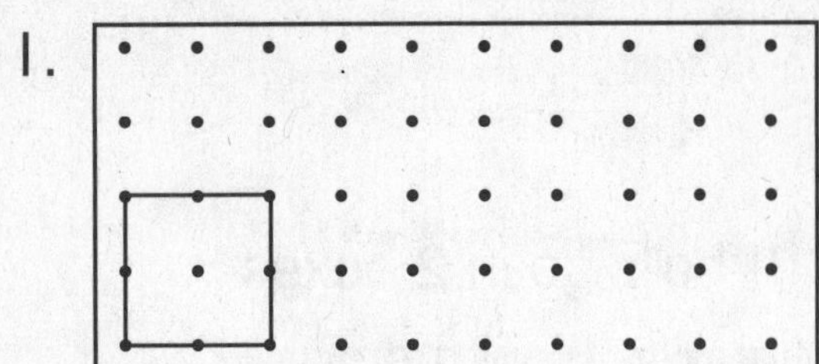

2. 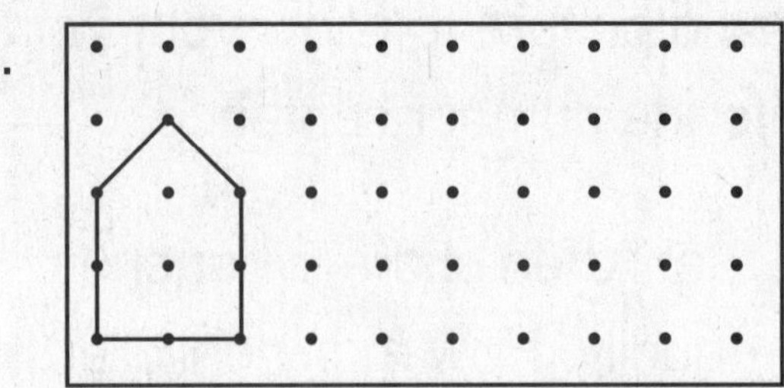

Problem Solving

3. Tasha cooked 30 hot dogs and 18 hamburgers at the picnic. How many lunches did she cook in all?

_____ lunches

4. At the picnic, there were 45 adults and 29 children. How many more adults were there than children?

_____ adults

Getting Ready for Next Year

Copy each problem on a seperate piece of paper. Add.

5.

11	25	33	24	46	18
12	14	10	15	21	19
+ 13	+ 3	+ 29	+ 17	+ 16	+ 20

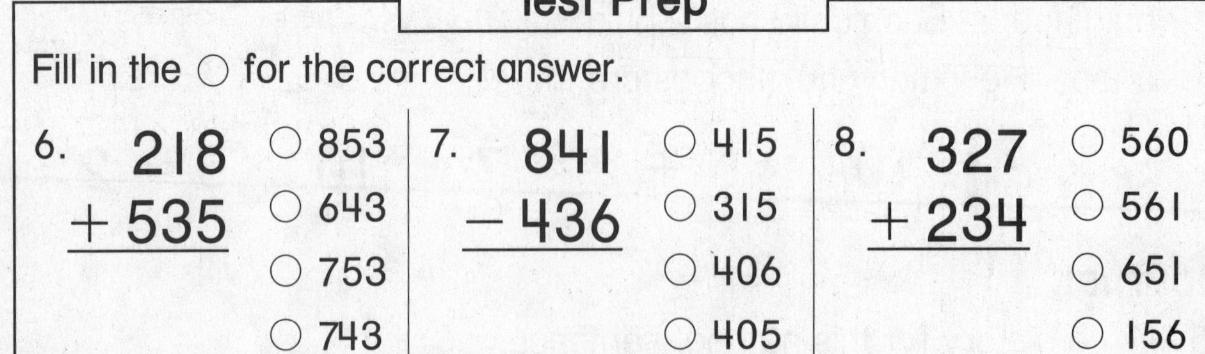

Test Prep

Fill in the ○ for the correct answer.

6. 218 + 535
○ 853
○ 643
○ 753
○ 743

7. 841 − 436
○ 415
○ 315
○ 406
○ 405

8. 327 + 234
○ 560
○ 561
○ 651
○ 156

Notes for Home Your child reviewed congruence, addition, subtraction, and word problems.
Home Activity: Draw a shape. Ask your child to draw a shape that is congruent, or has the same shape and size.

 Use with page 518.